YOUR KNOWLEDGE HAS

- We will publish your bachelor's and master's thesis, essays and papers

- Your own eBook and book - sold worldwide in all relevant shops

- Earn money with each sale

Upload your text at www.GRIN.com
and publish for free

Thomas Niedermeier

Vergleich des Risikoverständnisses in den Disziplinen Wirtschaftsinformatik und Soziologie

Comparison of the risk understanding in the disciplines Information Systems and Sociology

GRIN Publishing

Imprint:

Copyright © 2010 GRIN Verlag GmbH
Print and binding: Books on Demand GmbH, Norderstedt Germany
ISBN: 978-3-640-76422-8

This book at GRIN:

http://www.grin.com/en/e-book/162186/vergleich-des-risikoverstaendnisses-in-den-disziplinen-wirtschaftsinformatik

GRIN - Your knowledge has value

Since its foundation in 1998, GRIN has specialized in publishing academic texts by students, college teachers and other academics as e-book and printed book. The website www.grin.com is an ideal platform for presenting term papers, final papers, scientific essays, dissertations and specialist books.

Visit us on the internet:

http://www.grin.com/

http://www.facebook.com/grincom

http://www.twitter.com/grin_com

FAKULTÄT FÜR INFORMATIK
DER TECHNISCHEN UNIVERSITÄT MÜNCHEN

Bachelorarbeit in Wirtschaftsinformatik

Comparison of the risk understanding in the disciplines Information Systems and Sociology

Vergleich des Risikoverständnisses in den Disziplinen Wirtschaftsinformatik und Soziologie

Author: Thomas Niedermeier

Submission Date: 15. September 2010

Abstract

In the sociology of risk, there are two different fields of research: risk objectivism and risk constructivism. The former deals with the actual increase of danger due to greater pressures through new technologies. Risk constructivism deals with the conception, perception and evaluation of risks in the social environment. Beck is a representative of objectivism. In his view, risk is produced by modern society itself. New risks are constantly emerging as a result of technological progress. This means that humans create their own risk environment and must now deal with it.

Luhmann sees risk from a systems theory perspective. A social system is a process of social interactions between acting entities. According to Luhmann, risk only arises when there is communication about it. Furthermore, Luhmann sees the distinction between risk and safety as misleading and illusory. He proposes the concept of risk and danger. Douglas and Wildavsky represent neither an objective nor constructive notion of risk. They see risk as a collective construct that is shaped by the social context of the respective actors. The perception of risk is a social process. With the help of the grid-group model, a society can be divided into four cultural forms with specific risk-related characteristics. The cultural forms are individualism, hierarchy, fatalism and egalitarianism.

The understanding of risk in information systems is analyzed based on software project management and IT security.

The challenge in software development is to find the best position between costs and performances in order to satisfy both internal and external stakeholders. This is attempted with four approaches to risk management: risk checklists, an analysis framework, process models and risk response strategies. In this connection, it's worth noting that risks are perceived differently. Different risk assessments arise in various countries and different management levels.

In the area of IT security, the ranking of risks varies in different countries. This difference in ranking can be explained with the help of the technology threat avoidance theory. As such, the process of something such as technology risk will be perceived in a clearer manner. The evaluation of the consequences and information plays a role in countering the threat. There are also two sociological components. The first is the informal influence. "Informal" is the quantity of information that makes its environment available. The second, "normative" influence deals with social norms and demands that are used to counter the risk.

When comparing the notions of risk, one notices that Douglas' cultural approach to risk is transferable in information systems. The social environment influences the risk understanding of the employee and corporate risk culture. Employee and corporate risk culture influence each other. Furthermore we can found the different culture forms in information systems.

The various perceptions of risks are due to cultural aspects, amongst other things. Social values, ethics and philosophies influence our understanding of risk. If you combine various approaches such as risk management, security policies and strategies as well as employees' awareness of business risk management culture, another unique culture is created. This is influenced by and interactive with the surrounding sociological culture.

Keywords: Social risk theory, risk sociology, IT security risk, software project risk

Table of Content

List of Figures

List of Tabel

List of Abbreviations

AACE	Association for the Advancement of Computing in Education
ACM	Association for Computing Machinery
BSE	Bovine spongiforme Enzephalopathie
BSI	Bundesamt für Sicherheit in der Informationstechnik
CSI	Combat Studie Institute
IEEE	Institute of Electrical and Electronics Engineers Inc.
IS	Information Systems
IT	Information technology
MIS	Management Information Systems
MIT	Massachusetts Institute of Technology
PC	Personal computers
SRM	Security risk management
TTAT	Technology Threat Avoidance Theory

1 Introduction and Organization

Nothing happens without risk, but without risk, nothing happens either. This is how the German politician and Federal President Walter Scheel described the situation regarding risk. Today's society is surrounded by risks. Be it the daily crossing of an intersection, driving or work-related decisions with an uncertain outcome, each person is more or less confronted with significant risks on a daily basis. Businesses must make daily decisions that are associated with risks. Any decision that affects the future is a risk.

In computer sciences, new technologies are developed and existing technologies are further developed. This brings both new opportunities as well as challenges. Hacker attacks, spyware, viruses, spoofing, phishing, social engineering or even greater forces such as fire or lightning surround our information technology (=IT) landscape.

Even in project management - or, more specifically, software project management – there are risks of a much different nature. Software projects are high-risk activities, generating variable performance outcomes (Charette 2005, 1-7).

In the following paper, the understanding of risk in sociology and information systems is identified. It is divided into three main points. First, the understanding of risk in sociology is analyzed. Here, we will look at different concepts of risk sociology. We first consider the cultural approach of Douglas and Wildavsky. The culture forms the basic framework of the risk. We then consider the views of Beck and Luhmann. Both representatives see the risk or the increase in risk as being due to the rising number of problems from new technologies. New technologies are a big challenge in the areas of IT security and software project management. Finally, we will analyze the risk perspective from a socio-political point of view. Foucault sees risk as a government strategy for forceful control that results in the society being monitored and managed according to neoliberalist policies. This societal guidance can be transferred to general risk management in the areas of IT security and project management.

The second main point is the understanding of risk in information systems. We will therefore initially consider the project risks. In doing so, we only observe the software project development. Compared to portfolio projects or program projects, software projects have a unique character and are temporary. Risks can be easily analyzed and directly linked with their effects. The effect of coordinating projects is less complex with unique software projects. The second point of view that we look at is the field of IT Security. Technology poses an especially significant risk in this field.

As a final major point, we compare the two views. In doing so, we try to both transfer sociological concepts to information systems and rediscover sociological ideas in information systems. The cultural risk approach plays an important role in this process.

2   Understanding of Risk in Sociology

Sociological risk research describes the relationship between risk and society. From a scientific standpoint, there are two different perceptions in this regard: risk objectivism and risk constructivism. The former deals with the actual increase of danger. This increase in danger is attributed to rising objective pressure through new technologies. Risk constructivism deals with the conception, perception and evaluation of risks in the social environment. Risk is perceived by means of a social filter and evaluated in a social context (Tacke 2000, 1).

Controversial viewpoints create an area of tension between risk objectivism and risk constructivism, but current risk research is attempting to overcome this hurdle. However, the fact is that both theoretical approaches influence the understanding of risk. We will therefore look at different approaches to the sociological understanding of risk in the following paper. We will examine approaches by Ulrich Beck, Mary Douglas and Aaron Wildavsky as well as Niklas Luhmann. In this connection, Beck represents the risk objectivism approach. Douglas and Wildavsky follow a constructive socio-cultural approach to risk.

Ekberg (Ekberg 2007, 348) distinguishes between real and socially constructed risks. The tangible construed notion of risk sees risk as a daily occurrence. Thus, risks can be identified, measured, classified and reproduced. On the other hand, the socially construed notions of risks assume that there are no risks; only the social analysis of reality comes to light. For example, the cultural theory risk approach as according to Douglas would be valid in this case. The notion of risk society as according to Beck and Giddens contains elements of both approaches.

Ekberg (Ekberg 2007, 3ff) developed a conceptual model that identifies six characteristics of risk society concepts. They include
1. ubiquity of risks and the formation of a collective understanding of risk
2. various understandings of risk
3. various definitions of risk
4. the origin of reflexivity as an individual and institutional answer to risk-related questions.
5. the inverse relationship between risk and trust
6. political dimension of the risk which links risks based on power and knowledge with political values.

2.1 The concept of risk society from Ulrich Beck

Ulrich Beck, Professor of Sociology at the Ludwig Maximilian University of Munich, is the co-founder of the concept of risk society. In his first work, "Risikogesellschaft" (Beck 1986) Beck defined the concept of risk society. He recognizes societies that are being threatened by major risks. Major risks are summarized as being natural risk (natural disasters), radioactivity and social risk (unemployment and globalization). In this connection, the risk of modern society itself is created. Beck describes this process as second or reflexive modernity. Unlike first modernity, which took place during the industrial revolution, second modernity sees risks being self-caused on a global level. This is where established problem solving approaches reach their limits.

This means that humans create their own risk environment and must now deal with it. Due to theological progress, new risks are constantly emerging. Oftentimes, these risks are not even detected by humans. These risks are consciously received and tolerated. However, dangers are viewed as a threat. Beck cites the process of individualization as a reason for the emergence of risks. A component of individualization includes the individual's transition from heteronomy to self-determination. This individualization process is divided into three dimensions (Beck 1986, 206ff). They include the

1. liberation
2. disenchantment
3. control and reintegration

dimension.

The liberation dimension is reflected in the "separation from historically prescribed social methods and relationships" (Beck 1986, 206). This means that one can break out of the social structures and group relationships that they are born into. The disenchantment dimension describes "the loss of traditional securities in terms of practical knowledge, beliefs and guiding standards" (Beck 1986, 206). The loss of this security creates a new form of freedom for the individual. The tradition's functions simultaneously lead to a new form of risk. The third and final dimension, the control and reintegration dimension, is the countermovement to the first two dimensions. It serves a compensating function to keep the social structure balanced.

Modern global risks can be characterized as
- delocalization,
- unpredictable,
- and non-compensable

in the time reflex modernity (Beck 2009, 3f) .

With delocalization, the point of origin and the effect are not geographically bound. Oftentimes, the origin can be local and the effects can be global. Unpredictable describes the unpredictability of risks. This is based on missing information and ignorance. The non-compensable characteristic is the last feature of global risks. Technological progress and dangers could still be compensated in the first modernity. This, for example, was achieved through increased safety standards in vehicles or manufacturing. However, this assumes that these risks are known. In reflexive modernity, the compensation of risks is replaced through preventive measures and obeisance. One deals with risks that neither predictably nor previously lead to losses.

These global risks - such as the financial crisis or global warming - have these attributes. These risks are not limited by space or time (both its start and duration). From a social point of view, this status means that no allocation of cause and consequence can be carried out. Global risks open a new moral and political space that leads to a culture of civil responsibility. The fact that everyone is vulnerable nowadays and that consequences affect us all describes the multidimensionality of these risks. Now add the complexity of it all. The financial crisis or global warming can no longer be regulated by individuals, groups or states. They concern the entire world population and must be solved cooperatively. This cooperation means that we need to work with responsible people that, given different circumstances, we otherwise wouldn't have had anything to do with.

Moreover, the concepts of risk / danger and disaster must be differentiated. Risk cannot be put on a level with disaster. Danger is the anticipation of a disaster (Beck 2006, 4). Only when the danger has occurred does it actually become a disaster.

In connection with the new risks, Beck created the "new cosmopolitanism" and "organized irresponsibility" concepts (Beck 2009, 5ff). Under new cosmopolitanism, Beck understands that "global risks confront us with the others that are excluded" (Beck 2007). Cosmopolitanism should describe the transformation process from the first modernity to the second modernity. While in the first modernity, industrial society, an international order and a homogeneous national culture turns to a second modernity, in which the traditional problem solving mechanisms fail (Köhler 2006, 50). With regard to risks, this is how national borders become unimportant and how problems outside of our borders become our own problems. Other people's problems no longer exist because these problems affect everyone. This means that problems must be solved in an international context.

Organized irresponsibility is the situation in which a society cannot adequately handle unforeseeable events, negative consequences and long-term damage even though suitable institutions and control devices exist (Asselt/Vos 2008, 1-2). Science constantly expands the scope of action through new knowledge and ignorance, yet it has no solutions available on how to handle the resulting increase in risks (Münch 2002, 423). As such, damage to the economy is not taken over by the economy itself. Scientists are only responsible for technological (Yates 2001, 6) opportunities, but not for their implementation. Society is the laboratory for the outcome of the experiment.

4

Even our modern institutions of science, politics and business are overwhelmed with the new risks. The social perception of these institutions changes from rationally donating expert institutions to suspicious establishments. They are no longer viewed as an institution of risk management but rather as a source of danger. This loss of confidence in the expert system leads to an individualization process. This results in individuals no longer trusting these institutions. However, they have no choice but to trust them.

2.2 Risk as a Collective Construct from the Culture

Douglas and Wildavsky see risk in the context of different groups - this is what fundamentally distinguishes them from Beck. This is expressed in Cultural Theory, where risk is perceived as a collective construct that is shaped by the social context of the respective actors. Thus, the perception of risk is a social process that leads from an objective risk to a subjective perception of risk. Douglas and Wildavsky have a basic assumption that the quantity of risks and potential dangers amongst modern societies are not individually documented. Selected risks are chosen through the social fabric and are only perceived by the individual.

The socio-cultural risk approach involves two lines of research, as discussed below. One is Douglas' description of society's perception of danger (Douglas 1966, 1-12) while the other is the grid-group model (Douglas 2002, 54-69 ; Douglas 1978).

Douglas understands endangerment as being caused by the cultural view of danger. Culture helps individuals begin to understand risks. Culture purports which consequences and losses from society are assessed in a serious or trivial manner. With this perspective, ethical and moral constructs enter social risk assessment.

The grid-group model (see Figure 1) consists of two dimensions and is used to classify forms of social organization. The grid dimension is the vertical axis and provides information on the regulations of societies. This includes the experience of classifications about set norms, role expectations and functions (Krohn/Krücken 1993, 3). The grid axis provides information regarding the question of whether my social situation is determined by comprehensive rules, or if I have enough freedom to enforce my own behavior.

The horizontal Group axis describes the cohesion in the group. It is a measure of the feeling of togetherness that arises in the group. It provides information on whether an individual belongs to an existing social unit, or if they create their own social network (Caulkins 1999, 4ff). This is where a society's degree of differentiation from another society and its distinction in its moral concepts is expressed (Douglas/Wildavsky 1982, 138).

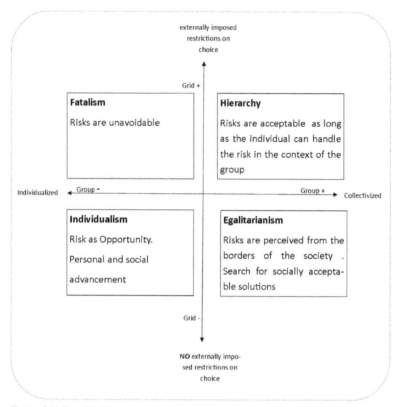

Figure : Grid-Group Model
Source: Adapted from (Caulkins 1999, 5 ; Schwarz/Thompson 1990, 7 ; Renn 1991, 8)

These two dimensions can each have high or low values. The resulting fields in the cross-classified table describe four ideal types of cultural forms (Vaughan 2002, 4f):

Individualism, hierarchy, egalitarianism, fatalism.

In *individualism*, there is neither strong group bonding nor control through rules. Questions regarding the coordination and resolving of problems are processed according to a market-based solution, without consideration for the individual person. In this context, market-oriented means that the society decides to search for a solution to the risks and sets self-regulating measures on the market. Specific individuals are trusted more than organizations (Lupton 1999, 51). In doing so, no regulatory or controlling authority is used. Even moral values are not included in the solution.

6

With the *hierarchy* form, individuals are subject to strong group control and regulatory codes of conduct. Risks are considered acceptable as long as the individual can handle the risk in the context of the group. Blame is not pushed on the group structure itself, as it's distributed to several members of the group.

With *egalitarianism*, there is a high degree of solidarity between the individuals. However, they have fewer possibilities to exert control. Douglas described this characteristic as being that of a cult. Risks are primarily perceived from the borders of the society and beyond. Blame is sought outside the group. The presence of external threats, in turn, strengthens the solidarity of the group.

Fatalism and egalitarianism are two side issues. Fatalistic cultural manifestations occur when there is a high degree of external control with an existing form of group exclusion. Members are bound to a system with many rules that they can't exercise any power over. They are helpless   with   risks   and   problems   due   to   the   high   grid   density. On the other hand, there is egalitarianism.

"[The increase in social awareness of technical and ecological risks is attributed to the institutional stabilization of this movement. It is in a permanent conflicting relationship with the semantics of market risk and hierarchy and forces society to exercise far-reaching perceptive changes and revaluations]" (Krohn/Krücken 1993, 3).

2.3   Risk in the Context of Communications and Systems Theory from Luhmann

In his book "Soziologie des Risikos" (Luhmann 1991), Luhmann views risk from the sociological approach to systems theory. He considers the question of why we deal with any risks at all in order to achieve the highly improbable. Luhmann presumes that this is based on a sociological systems theory approach. This approach goes back to the sociologist Talcott Parsons (Parsons 1991). He sees social systems as a process of social interactions between acting units. In this connection, the view of the order is placed within this interaction. In other words, each system has solid features and structures that are used to solve problems. Luhmann goes one step further. He doesn't see the system as a solid unit. In order to solve problems, social units communicate and interact with each other. This systems-based thinking attempts to reduce the complexity of the environment (Bergmans 2008, 3).

Luhmann defines risk (Luhmann 1991, 9-41) as being able to identify a decision that causes loss. This involves decisions that could possibly be regrettable in their early stages. One reaches a decision at a particular time, but it only reveals itself and its effects at a much later date.
At the same time, Luhmann nevertheless notes that there are no fixed definitions and perspectives that meet all requirements (Luhmann 1991, 27). Thus, there is no risk that must be discovered in order to avoid it. According to Luhmann, risk is initially constituted via the

communication of the risk. In other words, we don't recognize the risk at all if it isn't addressed by anyone.

Unlike Beck, who describes risk as a fundamental innovation due to technological progress, Luhmann sees a fundamental social change in the perception and handling of risks (Bergmans 2008, 4). Luhmann refers to three causes for this new kind of perception.

First, an increased dependence on society in the decision process: the society is aware that problems have many different solutions. Some are obvious, while others are less obvious. One can, however, only choose one solution. Thus, the person is dependent on their decision because the consequences of a false decision become increasingly clear.

Second, the importance of time: in modern society, we think in terms of "before" and "after". For us, the future is open and unpredictable.

Last cause is the difference between decision makers and affected persons.

On this basis, Luhmann tries to analyze what constitutes risk for parties within system-oriented communication processes (Metzner 2002, 262). In order to achieve this, the model of the second observer is used. Luhmann understands a second observer to be an objective person who observes how an observer observes. Second order observers see the object with different information that's based on their knowledge and ignorance; the observer shares the same perspective (Luhmann 1991, 30).

Using the second observer, Luhmann defined the difference between risk and safety as well as risk and danger. Risk is regarded as any possible loss that results from a decision. For him, security refers to when the impossibility of future losses can be asserted. This distinction between risk and safety is often used by security experts. With the help of facts and their interpretations, they try to maximize security. However, they do not understand that security is an illusion. There is no absolute security, as a decision's impact on the future is linked with uncertainty. Accordingly, Luhmann sees the distinction between risk and security as meaningless, since both are interdependent. Security experts acknowledge that there is no absolute security. The term "risk" is therefore used to specify its security efforts and scale in a reasonably calculated, accessible manner (Luhmann 1991, 28).

Luhmann proposes the distinction between risk and danger (Luhmann 1991, 27). By contrast, risk occurs when one can reduce the accountability of a loss to a personal decision or omission. This refers to a personal attribution in the system. Danger is the attribution of the loss to its external environment and consequent foreign attribution to another system. "[One can describe danger as being every negative effect that isn't too improbable in one's own sphere of life]" (Luhmann 1997, 327). Luhmann states that forces of nature are an example of the external environment. To illustrate the difference between the pairs of risk and danger, Luhmann refers to the umbrella example. The external, unalterable danger that we may get wet is converted into a risk when we decide to take an umbrella. This is called risk transformation (Luhmann 1997, 328). This is where another problem arises. With the possibility to make a decision to take the umbrella along, the real danger of getting wet or not is only shifted. The danger of getting wet is transformed into a risk through the previous decisions. With the onset of this transformation, there is no longer a danger but there is still a risk. However, from this point in time onward, one cannot live without risk. Risk perception and acceptance is dependent on whether an individual assesses an event as a risk or danger.

Nevertheless, risks are often assessed as being highly unlikely, yet the society assesses this risk as being extremely threatening. Luhmann explains this phenomenon with the disaster threshold. Disaster thresholds only accept events when they don't reach the threshold that is perceived as being a disaster. However, it is different from person to person.

At the same time, Luhmann deals with the distinction between affected persons and decision makers (Luhmann 1991, 114ff). People make decisions that don't only affect themselves. Thus, a decision maker is also responsible for other people. However, affected persons have no influence on the choice of the decision maker. If you include the complementary pair of risk and danger, the circumstances of the case can present a risk for the decision maker and a danger for the affected person (Luhmann 2003, 111-135).

Accountability is the problem. When accumulated decision-making effects or long-term effects don't have identifiable repercussions, it is difficult to attribute the consequences of a decision even though it's clear that without it, nothing would have happened.

There is no risk-free behavior – in other words, there's no such thing as absolute security. Consequently, one can only hope that more knowledge or better research will do a better job of merging risk and safety. True to the motto, the more you know, the more you know that you know nothing.

Preventing risks and threats is seen as "risk sharing strategies". Consequently, the first risk is intercepted because a second risk enters the fold. For example, during projects, managers are constantly trying to query data and information in order to control risk. However, this process only intends to confirm their initial decisive acceptance to the entry of the risk and thereby produce a pseudo-controllability.

2.4　　Risk and Govermantiality

For Foucault, the definition of risk is irrelevant. He merely states that there is a difference between the French "sécurité" and English "security" concepts of risk (Valverde 2007, 172) Risk is considered to be rationally calculative. Risk is viewed as a government strategy for forceful control that results in the society being monitored and managed according to neoliberalist policies. Foucault is concerned with issues such as how institutions and governments use force to lead the population.

Therefore, "government" not only refers to forms of political control or the structure of governmental bodies, but also to techniques and rationalities of the "leadership of people".

From this perspective, risks - as with Beck's analysis – do not comply with or depict real facts, but they produce social reality.

To understand Focault's followers and their understanding of risk, the term "gouvernementalité" must be explained. It goes back to Michel Foucault's lecture at the Collège de France. "Gouvernementalité" consists of the words "governer" and "mentalité", which means "thought". In summary, one can say that governmentality describes the art of leadership (Lemke 2006 ; Lemke 2002). This also addresses the leader's relationship with power and knowledge. The actions of leaders are influenced through knowledge and awareness. However, governmentality not only refers to the political and structural control of state authorities, but also to the techniques and rationality regarding the leadership of people (Lemke 2003, 2). Governmentality is about dividing life into different areas (Burchell/Gordon/Miller 1991, 96). Examples of these areas include institutions such as the economy, education, or disease. These institutions form the framework of neoliberal governance.

But how is risk seen through the eyes of Focault's followers? For them, risk is a form of social control (Lupton 1999, 87).

Contrary to Beck's self constructed risk society, Foucault has a sophisticated understanding of risk (Pearce/ Tombs 1996 1-15; Lemke 2000 1-16 ; Dean , 1999 176-189). Foucault and his researching coworker François Ewald don't see risk as being dangerous or disastrous, but rather as a predictable regularity. Ewald doesn't just consider risk to be something negative; he also sees it as being a positive opportunity.

For Francois Ewald's Foucault-based risk analyses, risks are not technologically or socially justified, but rather a specific type of social thinking about events. Accordingly, Ewald distinguishes risks as being calculable and incalculable. Thus, Ewald follows the insurance-based ideas of financial security. He even goes one step further and claims that targets are made deliberately because the insurance system wants to find ways to insure the uninsurable and thereby ungovernable (Ewald 1993, 210-211). Insurance is a political tool to compensate for losses through financial compensation. Consequently, it is more important for Ewald to deal with the technology of authority than to follow Beck's approach of dealing with the power of technology. This risk production has a social origin. It only becomes a social thematization through the narrative of risk. Accordingly, risk shouldn't be bound to reality, but rather to its thematization. Like Beck, Foucault sees the need for expert knowledge - however, he takes a different approach to it (Lupton 1999, 88ff). For him, experts serve to analyze risks and create guidelines and standards for society. Through this process, the government sees risks as being controllable or insurable.

According to Mitchell Dean (Dean 1998, 1) there is no risk. Risk is only a means to calculably organize reality. Through this order, it is controllable for the government.

3   Risks in Information Systems

This point we discuss the understanding of risk in information systems. We will therefore initially consider the project risks. In doing so, we only observe the software project development. Compared to portfolio projects or program projects, software projects have a unique character and are temporary. Risks can be easily analyzed and directly linked with their effects. The effect of coordinating projects is less complex with unique software projects. The second point of view that we look at is the field of IT Security. Technology poses an especially significant risk in this field.

3.1   Risks in Software Project Management

In this Chapter we first define the word project and project risks. Then we discuss the tradition Risk Management strategies and their influence on the project. We look on the product and process performance. Finally we identify the different risk factors and their observance in the eyes of employee and management.

3.1.1 Definition of Project, Project Risks and Some Categorization

To define project risks, we must first define the term "project". There are many different definitions to choose from. In summary, one can define the term "project" as follows: "A one-time, specific task to be accomplished within prescribed quality and economic parameters in a finite time period. Task should include a definition of desired end results containing measurable performance criteria" (Cabano 2004, 1). Having found a thorough definition for "project", it is now time to look at the concept of risk in relation to projects.

The broadest definition of risks in software projects is that the risks present a weighted probability of the occurrence of an event in a project (Boehm 1989, 2ff) (Boehm/Ross 1989, 7). This can be simplified by using the following formula: $R = P \times I$ (Bannerman 2008, 2). "R" represents the risk exposure to a particular risk factor. "P" specifies the probability of occurrence of an undesirable event and "I" specifies its magnitude in the actual occurrence of the event.

There are two classes of risks. Generic risks are dangers that affect all projects. They can be controlled with standard development techniques. Project-specific risks only occur in one particular aspect of the project. They require a specific risk management plan and profile.

From an organizational point of view, risks arise when organizations hesitantly pursue opportunities that are limited by cost and performance (Bannerman 2008, 2). The challenge is to find the optimal position between cost and efficiency and to satisfy both internal and external stakeholders.

3.1.2 Management Understanding of Risk and their Limitation

The risk-based understanding of information systems goes back to the management theory of the 80's (Bannerman 2008, 2). March and Shapira (March/Shapira 1987, 1-15) compared the traditional risk and decision theory with the decisions of managers from Canadian firms. At that time, risk was seen as a variation of the probability of a positive or negative result from a previous decision. Risk is still sometimes viewed in this light. 80% of managers only see negative consequences from risks. Results with a low probability are ignored due to a significance threshold. However, if the result has a significant consequential loss or risk, it falls back into the focus of the observer. Decisions with positive results are only linked with the decision-making alternatives. The best possible alternative is selected and a conclusion is drawn that it will have the most positive outcome. Managers float in the idea that they can control risk and that it therefore poses no danger. Risk perspective is not just a personal preference. Social norms and organizational expectations have a significant impact on the observer. As a result, the behavior of the manager is different from the management theory.

The findings of March and Shapira are transferred to software development. Bannerman (Bannerman 2008, 2-3) describes dealing with risk in software projects as identifying all possible risk factors before the project begins in order to reduce the probability of a negative result occurring. The identified risks are then estimated in order to find those with the most negative influence. These high risk factors are precisely controlled in order to avoid a potential loss. This process is constantly updated and maintained. However, risks can only be minimized by consulting predefined danger lists or by reaching a threshold. Bannerman sees four limitations based on this view of risk.

First, March and Shapira pointed out that this theoretical approach does not reflect the actual leadership behavior of managers. Managers are more concerned about the extent of a potential loss than its probability of occurrence. Verbal statements are preferred probabilistic representations. With their management skills and tools, they believe that risks can be controlled and mastered.

A second limitation of the risk concept is the difficulty of correctly assessing the impact of different risk factors. Probability is only useful only when there are multiple repetitions. This contradicts the unique nature of software development.

Third, risk event is coupled with risk result. As such, the organization-specific vulnerabilities and skills of execution and attenuation is ignored. Zhang (Zhang 2007, 1-7) sees vulnerability as the ability of an organization to react to dangers. In previous studies, only events and consequences were considered without the project itself. The project influences both situations.

The fourth and final limitation is the fact that only known and foreseeable risks are involved. Unrecognizable threats are not included.

3.1.3 Risk Management in Software Projects

First, there is the question of what risk mangement even is. In addition to a large number of definitions, risk management can be defined as follows: through various policies, principles and practices, the identification, analysis and handling of both predictable and unpredictable events should be improved in order to ensure a successful project progression (Bannerman 2008, 3 ; Boehm 1989, 2ff ; Boehm 1991, 2-9) and exit or to at least avoid project failure (Iversen/Mathiassen/Nielsen 2004, 7-10 ;Lewis/Watson/Pickren 2003, 2). Risk management can be practiced in various sectors (Hynuk et al. 2009, 1-31). The sectors are either project, program or portfolio-based. A program has a structure of multiple projects that are led in a coordinated manner in order to attain greater benefits (Pellegrinelli 1997, 1-8). In other words, a program is a temporary organization of several projects that are managed together in order to achieve a higher strategic goal that a single project otherwise wouldn't reach (Turnera/Müller 2003, 2-3). Portfolio project management involves managing several projects in order to achieve strategic goals. However, it's done with the help of various management processes in order to reduce the uncertainty of the portfolio (Turnera/Müller 2003, 4-5,7).

Next, we will solely deal with risk management in the software project sector.

The advantages to using risk management in software projects are that the focus is placed on different problematic situations, possible sources of error are emphasized, potential threats are linked with appropriate countermeasures and a common perception of the project is made possible amongst the employees (Kalle et al. 1998, 3-5 ; Lyytinen/Mathiassen/Ropponen 1996, 4ff).

In practice, the following four approaches to risk management are used: *risk checklists, analysis framework, process models* and *risk response strategies*. The following paragraphs will shed light on the various approaches (Bannerman 2008, 3-5 ; Iversen/Mathiassen/Nielsen 2004, 8-9).

Risk checklists are primarily attributed to strategic business management. With this instrument, events are checked with reference to a prepared list of known threats. In software project management, they include general elements of risk that aid the project manager in concentrating on possible sources of risk. They don't contain any information on effective countermeasures. They are therefore best geared towards risk assessment because they are easy to create, contain a great deal of experience value and are easily extendable (Iversen/Mathiassen/Nielsen 2004, 8). Bannerman finds that there are four problems with checklists (Bannerman 2008, 3-4).

First, there are several risk lists and each project has its own specific focus and problems. Projects are not uniform, so it is therefore difficult to generate a uniform project list. Second, the perception of risk changes in relation to the stakeholder group, project timeline and cultures. Third, project managers critically assess risks that are outside of their control area. The fourth and final problem is closely related to the assessment of the project manager. Project managers tend to worry more about the potential loss than the likelihood of occurrence. "However, risk surveys and checklists typically focus mainly on factors that contribute to the likelihood of project failure rather than on the magnitude of loss should failure" (Bannerman 2008, 4)

In addition to the risk checklists, the *Analysis Framework* model approach still exists in literature and in praxis. The individual risk checklists are still divided into risk categories and assessed on the basis of low and high scales. The basis for categorization is the perception or place of origin. By combining different risk lists, a wider range of risks can be captured and covered. Consequently, they are especially useful in the risk management process of identification and analysis. However, the problems that arise are similar to those with risk checklists. There are different framework approaches from which the appropriate approach has to be selected. Projects are still specific and frameworks try to generalize risks.

The third risk management approach is based on a process-oriented and gradual execution of various given tasks. *Process models* typically give specific activities for managing software development risks. The most sensible time-based sequence is also given. Some sub-processes can be supported with tools. In summary, all process models are essentially executed according to the following basic steps: risk strategy, risk identification, risk analysis, risk responses and risk control. The problem here is the lack of contextual knowledge. Although all of these models provide a good starting point for the identification and analysis of risks, they lack the analytical thinking that is needed to get a handle on the threat.

The last risk management approach is the *Risk Response Strategy*. With these comprehensive approaches, specific actions can be formulated depending which factor or type of threat is dominating the project. In addition, the removal of required costs and resources is considered. The reactions to a risk are to eliminate or reduce the probability its occurrence, limit the damage following the occurrence, or a combination of both. The following risk responses can be summarized: avoidance, transference, mitigation, acceptance. In spite of everything, even with process models, the reaction to unforeseeable problems remains excluded.

Iversen et al. (Iversen/Mathiassen/Nielsen 2004, 8-10) carries out a similar typification. He typecasts software risk management in risk list, risk action list, risk strategy models and risk strategy analysis. The risk lists are consistent with the view of Bannerman. The risk action list has prioritized risks with appropriate solutions. In addition to the risk list and action list, risk strategy models contain more abstract categories of risk and solutions. These categories are assessed on a high-low basis. Risk strategy analysis is as close as anything comes to risk response strategy.

3.1.4 Effect of Coordination and Uncertainty on Software Project Performance

Nidumolu (Nidumolu 1995, 1-7) argues that uncertainty in project management is due to poor coordination. Uncertainty is therefore a key issue for effective development. Both the vertical and horizontal coordination of software projects is therefore problematic in terms of the development's performance. With performance, Nidumolu understands both the process performance – it describes the process of development - and product quality performance. In his model, he examined the factors that influence the performance. It turned out that project uncertainty and residual performance risks have a direct negative impact. Residual performance risk is "defined as the extent of difficulty in estimating the performance-related outcomes of a project, regardless of the specific estimation technique used" (Nidumolu 1995, 5). As influencing factors for this risk, project uncertainty and vertical coordination are determined. The project uncertainties focus on two aspects. One is customer-based uncertainty in requirement engineering, while the other is technical uncertainty such as potential unknown technologies that are required for the realization of the project. Vertical coordination is the hierarchical delegation of work instructions. This is mainly done by the project manager. The investigation found that project uncertainty has a positive impact on residual performance risk, while there is a negative impact on vertical coordination.

3.1.5 Risk Categories and their Effect on Product and Process Performance

Wallace and Keil (Wallace/Keil 2004, 1-6 ; Keil et al. 1998, 1-8) divided risks into four categories and examined their effect on project results with regard to the product and process. It was confirmed that checklists for risk avoidance are present in many companies, but they are not implemented effectively in risk management strategies. This is because many of the connections between risks and their impact are unknown in relation to the project results. Through a simple categorization of these risks, the relationship can be clarified. Wallace and Keil categorized risks as follows: "customer-client", "scope and requirement", "execution" and "environment". For example, the "customer-client" risk category can include a lack of customer-based support for management or conflict and cooperation problems in the collaboration between the client and contractor. The "scope and requirement" section includes traditional software engineering requirement risks such the false, inaccurate, incomplete or misunderstood requirement analyses of the project. Undefined success criteria and a lack of purpose also fall under this section. Amongst other things, "execution" includes project complexity, faulty supervision and implementation of the project and a lack of knowledge on behalf of project managers and employees alike. The "environment" category includes both the internal and external environment of a company. This includes external companies or suppliers that are involved in the development process as well as the influence of organizational and political factors.

As a result of the investigation, it turned out that all of the risk categories except for "environment" are influential. The process factor, which represents the success of a project as based on budget and time, is mainly influenced by "scope and requirement" and "execution". Consequently, managers need to reduce or avoid these risk categories. The influential risk categories for the product itself are "customer-client", "scope and requirement" and "execution". In this connection, "execution" has the greatest influence on the developed product. It was also noted that some risks are classified with more criticism than others. These risks mainly lie outside of the project manager's direct control (Keil et al. 1998, 7). The less control that a project manager has over a risk, the more they will see it as being dangerous.

3.1.6 Critical Risks in Outsourced IT projects

More and more software projects are outsourced to overseas companies. New risks arise through offshore outsourcing (Hazel 2006, 1-6). The project manager must deal with new and unknown risks that are rarely if ever used in traditional outsourcing projects. Hazel noted that a simple risk list alone doesn't lead to a successful project (Hazel 2006, 2). It is much more important to know which possible risks will cause problems because they are either difficult to compensate or difficult to predict. Hazel distinguished two types of risks: intractable and unforeseen risks. Intractable risks are those which, despite the manager's best efforts, are present from the onset. These particularly include risks that are related to time and budget management as well as those that deal with problems with new technology. All three risks arise due to inadequate preliminary analysis of the project.

Unforeseen risks are problems that are either not recognized or classified as being unlikely. Thus, no provision is made for these problems, which particularly include the relationship between the client and contractor. Customer confidence, customer expectations and change management are amongst the most mentioned problem categories. Due to their elusive nature, they are especially difficult to qualify. Oftentimes, they first arise at a later point in time during the collaboration.

Iavcovou and Naktasu believe that a project can only have a successful outcome if the risk profile is clearly identified (Iacovou/Nakatsu 2008, 1-7). Altogether, the two authors divide the risks into three groups: the communication between contractors and clients, customers within project management and contractor skills. In communications, the main risk factors include miscommunication, language and cultural barriers as well as a lack of consultation in change management. The customer-specific risks include a lack of commitment from top management, inadequate customer involvement and problems in dealing with the end-user. Specific problems that arise in offshore outsourcing reveal themselves when it comes to know-how and in the calculation of total costs. The final risk category deals with contractor skills. "Skills" refers to both technical and business know-how. In summary, offshore projects are inherently risky ventures. They combine traditional project risks with new and unknown risks related to offshore outsourcing.

3.1.7 Risk Factors, Categories and their Observance

Through a large-scale study, Schmidt et al. (Schmidt et al. 2001, 1-33) examined the risk factors and their observance of software projects. They see the software project management process as having two phases: risk assessment and control measures. In turn, the risk assessment is divided into a further three phases. To begin with, the risk factor must be identified. A potential risk of loss is then determined for each risk factor. In the last step, the overall risk can be determined. The critical point in all of this is identifying the risk factor. A poor or incomplete identification of the risk factor results in poor risk management. Two different methods have emerged for risk identification: the checklist method and the success factor method. The checklist is attributed to Barry W. Boehm (Boehm 1991, 1-10). He identified ten fundamental sources of risk in the software development process. In addition to the checklist method, there is the success factor method. With the success factor method, one attempts to identify factors that affect the project positively. As a result of their investigation, an extended risk factor list was comprised – it includes cultural and socioeconomic differences in various countries. The second part of the investigation focuses on the perception of risks. As such, software risks are divided into two categories: outside risks and inside risks. Outside risks are risks that the project manager cannot control because they lie outside of his/her sphere of influence. Amongst other things, they include conflicts between departments, the number of linked organizational units or new subject matter. On the other hand, inside risks can be controlled and monitored. A few examples include misunderstandings in requirement engineering or undefined end-user expectations. Between inside risk and outside risk, there is still a mixed form of both. It can be discovered by the project manager but is only subject to a small amount of influence or control. The introduction of new technology falls into this category. Although the project manager can prepare and train accordingly, there is still a residual risk towards the project's success. Overall, one can see that the greater the classification of the risks, the less influence the project manager has over them. However, when viewed from another angle, risks that fall under the category of inside risk are often given a low rating - this could lead to the actual risk being underestimated.

Another topic that Schmidt et al. (Schmidt et al. 2001, 1-33) addresses is the different levels of risk in different countries. The study was conducted in the USA, Finland and Hong Kong. Each of these countries has its own culture and risk avoidance. It therefore stands to reason that the views and rankings of risks are different. This was confirmed during the investigations. In cultures with a collective philosophy, risks are not attributed to the individual. Hong Kong consequently has fewer risks that a project manager is responsible for than the USA or Finland. In Hong Kong, more dangers tend to be viewed as being external as opposed to being under the control of the individual. This in turn leads to a different perception of risk.

Even the ranking related to the skills of the project manager is different between the cultures. Hong Kong and, in part, the USA represent a relatively "masculine" culture that doesn't accept personal shortcomings. In contrast, Finland's culture is more self-critical and less masculine. Socioeconomic elements also have an influence on this perception. In Hong Kong, managers often have to deal with personnel changes. Consequently, they – unlike Americans or Finns - estimate the risk of staff turnover to be controllable. In summary, one can say that both cultural and socioeconomic factors influence the identification and perception of different risk factors.

Tsetlin and Winkler (Tsetlin/Winkler 2005) ordered project risks as project risks and background risks and examined their correlation. Project risks are uncertainties that are directly connected with the project. Background risks are all of the other exogenous uncertainties that affect the decision-maker in his/her judgments. For example, these include exchange rates or taxes on the earnings of projects that are outside of the mother country. Even negative experiences from past projects are included in background risks. Background risks may either have an additive or multiplicative influence on the decision-makers.

3.1.8 Contingency Model of Software Project Risk Management

Baraki et al. (Baraki/Rivard/Talbot 2001, 1-34) developed a contingency model for software project risk management. Accordingly, the result is significantly influenced by matching project risks with how the project is managed. The project management profile must therefore be adjusted to the specific project risks in order to produce the best possible end result. The model has four dimensions: risk exposure, risk management, fit and project performance (See Figure 2).

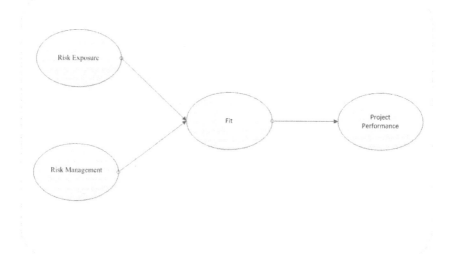

Figure : General Contingency Model of Software Project Risk Management
Source: (Baraki/Rivard/Talbot 2001, 7)

"Risk exposure is defined as this probability multiplied by the loss potential of the unsatisfactory outcome" (Baraki/Rivard/Talbot 2001, 7). Project sizes, technological innovation, skills, complexity and the organizational environment are assigned to this dimension (Baraki/Rivard/Talbot 2001, 12-14).

Risk exposure corresponds to risk management. Barki et al. understand risk management or the risk management profile to be "the profiles of the various approaches, tools, techniques, devices, or mechanisms utilized in managing a software project, and is therefore conceptualized as such in the present study" (Baraki/Rivard/Talbot 2001, 8). Overall, the risk management profile can be divided into in three dimensions or approaches: formal planning, internal integration and user participation.

Fit indicates the degree of interaction between risk exposure and the risk management profile.

Performance describes how efficiently and effectively the software project is created. As such, process performance and product performance can be distinguished. In this connection, process describes the course of development, while product performance describes the quality of the resulting software. It should be noted that a low process performance can yield a high product performance and vice versa. For example, a project that exceeds a timeline or budget plan and therefore has a low process performance can still yield a high quality product.

The study reveals that the interaction between the project management profile and risk exposure results in the "fit", which in turn has a significant impact on performance. However, there is no uniform management profile. A high level of risk exposure requires a different or higher risk management profile than with lesser risks. If one observes the process performance based on its budget, it turns out that high risk exposure requires a higher degree of internal integration and formal planning than lower projects. The project manager should therefore regularly communicate with his/her employees about adhering to timelines and goals. The project manager should also monitor his/her employees by complying with and using formal planning tools.

By observing the product performance as based on the quality of the final product, a high user participation results. The project manager can achieve this by giving his/her employees a greater sense of responsibility and an active role in the project.

3.1.9 Risk Perception and Risk Propensity on the Decision to Continue a Project

Keil et al. (Keil, et al. 2000, 1-10) studied the influence of risk perception and risk propensity on the project manager's decisions in software development. Risk propensity is a general characteristic that is uniquely pronounced with everyone. Some people look for risk, while others are more likely to select actions that entail little risk. Furthermore, risk tolerance is dependent on the respective situation (Maccrimmon/Wehrung 1985, 1-29). Other research (Brockhaus 1980, 1-11 ; Vleka/Stalle 1980, 1-28) showed that apart from their influence on the decision, risk propensity and risk perception still have a mutual interdependence. For example, people with a high risk tolerance tend to underestimate risks. They therefore weigh a situation by considering all of the possible positive results rather than dwelling on the probability of loss. This overestimation leads to a lower risk perception.

However, Keil et al. found that risk perception is very significantly correlated with the decision, yet curiously not with the risk tolerance. The risk perception of the project manager is more important than its tolerance. Accordingly, risk assessment tools should reduce the observer's various risk perceptions in order to achieve a similar result.

3.2   Risks in the Field of IT Security

Information technology has two sides: a good and a bad one. Without a doubt, a few of the positive elements include progress, simplification, optimization and improvement – the list can be endless. However, there is a downside. Information technology poses a threat to individuals, organizations and societies. Modern attacks such as viruses, worms, trojans, email spam or spyware present a serious threat to both home users and organizations. They cause great damage and financial losses (Bagchi/Udo 2003, 7-10). In Combat Studie Institute (=CSI) reports, the most expensive incidents in the field of IT security are those which are related to financial fraud (Richardson 2008, 6). The damage from 522 surveyed units was 500,000 U.S. dollars. The average loss amongst investigated units is 350,000 U.S. dollars. The worldwide financial impacts of malware increased from 3.3 trillion U.S. dollars in 1996 to 13.3 trillion in 2006 (Computer Economics 2007). The trend is constantly increasing.

3.2.1 Development and Progress of IT Security: From Past to Present

Dlaminia et al. (Dlaminia/Eloffa/Eloffb 2009, 1-10) divided the history of computer security into the past, present and future.

The telegraph was invented in 1840. Since then, the security aspect of news has changed from simply securing a letter to securing communication links for telegraphs and eventually protecting the news over the World Wide Web.

The field of IT Security began with the invention of the first generation of computers between 1940 and 1950. Back then, the security concerns involved insuring that only authorized personnel could run commands on the computer and making sure that the computer didn't get stolen or damaged. Computer security was limited to physical security. Data exchange was limited to physical media. This also required special attention to ensure that the data carrier wasn't damaged or lost.

Computer terminals arrived in the late 60's and 70's. With the help of the terminals, people could access remote data. Since then, the primary risk has revolved around unauthorized people accessing data. The physical safeguards that were available were sufficient. Next, authentication and identification came into play. This led to the development of digital signatures and public key cryptography in the early 70's. With the advent of personal computers (PC's) in the 80's, the number of computers that were being manufactured increased drastically. The user's knowledge also increased at an accelerated pace. This decade is characterized by viruses and worms such as "Elk Clonder" or "The Brain". The first anti-virus software was developed in the late 80's. The 90's are characterized by mobile computers and open systems like Unix. Whether mobile or stationary, more and more PC's were connected to the Internet. This brought new risks with it. Through the Internet, viruses and worms spread rapidly. Hacking tools became available for a vast number of experienced and inexperienced users.

At the end of the 90's, the behavior of attackers changed. Viruses and worms were replaced with more sophisticated techniques. Distributed denial of service and malicious code was distributed through web pages and emails. Firewalls were developed to combat these attacks. They are supposed to isolate the company from its environment. Dlaminia assessed this development from the 40's until the late 90's as follows: "However, the fact remains that all these new developments in technology were vulnerable and like all other good things came with side effects (risks)" (Dlaminia/Eloffa/Eloffb 2009, 3).

The 21st century has seen the initiation of a new dimension of IT security. Dlaminia et al. (Dlaminia/Eloffa/Eloffb 2009, 3) describes that the motivation for today's attacks tends to be based on financial interests. In order to avoid legal proceedings, everything is done to erase any possible traces. In the early days, attacks were carried out by computer enthusiasts.

Today, the approach is professionally and strictly organized. Viruses and worms can have catastrophic effects by infecting one thousand PC's within seconds. Spam and phishing are common occurrences with different communication channels such as email, SMS (short message service) and MMS (multimedia message service). An analysis of current topics in IT security by Dlaminia et al. (Dlaminia/Eloffa/Eloffb 2009, 6-9) resulted in the following: encryption and the handling of lost mobile devices is becoming increasingly important. Risk management is shifting from a tactical direction to a strategic one. Today's organizations must be more adaptable and flexible when it comes to dealing with risk. This approach encompasses people, processes and technology risks.

Loch et al. describes the history of IT security similarly (Loch/Carr/Warkentin 1992, 2-3). In the past, security was limited to the safeguarding of storage facilities, materials and money. In today's age of information technology, this outlook is undergoing a fundamental change. One of the most important assets of a company is its data. The backup of data is what actually poses the greatest danger these days. At the beginning of the threat of spyware, viruses and so on, only a few specialists knew about the defective application of certain technologies. Nowadays, physical security is no longer sufficient. Thanks to the Internet, threats exist everywhere. Furthermore, end users' technological knowledge has increased. This knowledge can be applied both positively and negatively. As a result companies find both themselves and their data in an extreme environment. The treats in this environment aren't only human. Natural disasters can create unpredictable consequences as well. Storms and hurricanes can bring complete communication links and energy supplies to a standstill.

Loch et al. describes the current threat as follows: "We tend to equate risk with something done to us. Natural disasters disrupt our power, our ability to produce, or our transportation capability. Less obvious is the risk we create in our actions, such as the installation of a new computer-based system, distribution of our processing and data storage across a country or world, or, as in the case of the banking industry, the movement from batch processing to telecommunications intensive real-time online processing" (Loch/Carr/Warkentin 1992, 2).

3.2.2 Categorization of IT Security Threats

Loch et al (Loch/Carr/Warkentin 1992, 1-5) divide IT Security risks according to their place of origin, perpetrator, intent and consequences (see Figure 3).

First, a distinction between an internal and external source. The company itself is what's meant regarding the place of origin. Internal means that the threat is within the company. This includes employee conduct, errors in business processes or the company's external environment. External threats originate outside of the company. These include natural disasters such as fires, floods, earthquakes or hurricanes. Other sources include competitors and hackers that try to access or damage relevant data.

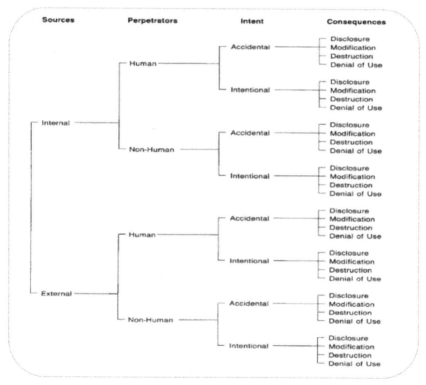

Figure : The Categorization of IT Security Threats
Source: (Loch/Carr/Warkentin 1992, 4)

Next, IT threats can be distinguished according to their initiator. Threats can therefore be of a human or nonhuman nature. This classification can only be problematic with viruses. They

22

are written and spread by people, but they act independently. Loch et al. nevertheless assigned them to the human category.

The initiators can in turn be divided into intentional or accidental threats. For example, computer viruses are intentionally written in order to generate a certain effect on a system, user or organization. Program errors are usually due to failures by the developer. The consequences of an attack can be divided into disclosure, modification, destruction and denial of use.

3.2.3 Ranking and Perception of IT Threats

Loch et al. (Loch/Carr/Warkentin 1992, 1-15) examined the perception of risk in the areas of microcomputers, mainframes and networks. In all three areas, natural disasters and accidental injuries caused by employees were considered the most dangerous. Risks within an organization are classified more critically than outside threats. It's also not surprising that the security dangers with are greater with microcomputers than with mainframe computers. The network within the company is classified as being very safe. Only the network connections that go outside are critically or uncertainly classified. It's interesting that the respondents were aware of the risks and assessed them as being critical, yet they perceived their own business-related threats as being low. In addition, they reckon that their competition is more vulnerable than they are. It's a poor judgment call to assume that bad things only happen to other people.

Loch et al. came up with the following rankings:

1. Natural disasters
2. Accidental entry bad data by employees
3. Accidental destruction data by employees
4. Weak/ineffective controls
5. Entry of computer viruses
6. Access to system by hackers
7. Inadequate control over media
8. Unauthorized access by employees
9. Poor control of I/
10. Intentional destruction data by employees
11. Intentional entry bad data by employee
12. Access to system by competitors
13. Other threats

Whitman (Whitman 2004, 6-15) analyzed the threats and frequency with which threats appear in information security as well as which ones experience the greatest expenditure.

What resulted was the following weighted ranking (Whitman 2004, 7):

1. Deliberate software attacks
2. Technical software failures or errors
3. Act of human error or failure
4. Deliberate acts of espionage or trespass
5. Deliberate acts of sabotage or vandalism
6. Technical hardware failures or errors
7. Deliberate acts of theft
8. Forces of nature
9. Compromises to intellectual property
10. Quality of service deviations from service providers
11. Technological obsolescence
12. Deliberate acts of information extortion

In comparing Hole and Whitman's studies, you realize that there is a large correlation between the two. However, it is noticeable that the threat of natural disasters has been greatly reduced. Nevertheless, it is worth noting that even after more than twelve years, the ranking turns out to be relatively similar despite the further development of IT security measures. In examining the frequency of attacks during the evaluation period, the following ranking resulted (Whitman 2004, 8):

1. Act of human error or failure
2. Compromises to intellectual property
3. Deliberate acts of espionage or trespass
4. Deliberate acts of information extortion
5. Deliberate acts of sabotage or vandalism
6. Deliberate acts of theft
7. Deliberate software attacks
8. Forces of nature
9. Quality of service deviations from service providers
10. Technical hardware failures or errors
11. Technical software failures or errors
12. Technological obsolescence

What's striking here is that most of the threats are due to human failures or errors.

3.2.4 Risk Perception: The Technology Threat Avoidance Theory

With the help of the technology threat avoidance theory (TTAT), Liang and Xue (Liang/Xue 2009, 1-21) described the individual IT user's behavior in relation to IT risk avoidance. The perception of IT risks is incomplete. For example, in order to act against an email virus, the user must first perceive and realize that the virus is a threat. When choosing a course of action, the user has several options. He/she can enable the firewall, update the antivirus software or stop retrieving emails. A combination of these actions would be useful. However, if the user has only chosen to use anti-virus software, they won't consider all of the other available actions and alternatives. What's more is that in IT security, more value is placed on avoiding IT threats than implementing a specific IT safeguard. This phenomenon goes back to a fundamental difference between the behavior that's related to the acceptance or avoidance of risks (Carver/White 1994, 6-15 ; Elliot 2006, 1-6). This appearance of acceptance and avoidance of risks in IT is explained with the help of the technology threat avoidance theory (TTAT). The TTAT expands different approaches from business informatics, risk analysis, psychology and health. Liang and Xue see TTAT as a dynamic and positive feedback loop that can explain avoidance behavior by way of cybernetics (Wiener 1965, 144-169) and the coping theory. The central idea of cybernetics is that the people regulate their behavior on their own through feedback loops. In so doing, one distinguishes between a positive and negative feedback loop. A positive feedback loop occurs when a variable has a reinforcing effect on itself. The negative feedback loop weakens the variable. The phenomenon of risk avoidance can therefore be seen as a positive feedback loop (Liang/Xue 2009, 5)

With the TTAT (see Figure 4 next page), the user follows a divided cognitive process in order to assess risks. First, it's the IT *threat appraisal* and *coping appraisal* process and then *Coping* the follows.

With IT *threat appraisal*, the user evaluates the possible negative consequences of malicious software. A threat is only perceived as based on a certain threshold. Threat appraisal is directly influenced by perceived susceptibility and perceived severity. "Perceived susceptibility is defined as an individual's subjective probability that the malicious IT will negatively affect him or her, and perceived severity is defined as the extent to which an individual perceives that negative consequences caused by the malicious IT are severe. Only when users believe that they are vulnerable to malicious IT and that the consequence of being attacked is serious will they perceive a threat" (Liang/Xue 2009, 10) "Perceived severity is defined as the extent to which an individual perceives that negative consequences caused by the malicious IT are severe. Only when users believe that they are vulnerable to malicious IT and that the consequence of being attacked is serious will they perceive a threat" (Liang/Xue 2009, 10). To illustrate the difference, we take a virus that formats the hard drive and a spyware that collects information about the user. The virus attack is classified as disastrous because it suggests that all data will be lost. However, the spyware attack is seen as being rather harmless. The consequential damages only reveal themselves after some time. The number of users also has an influence on the perception. The more users there are that believe they are vulnerable to a threat, the greater the risk perception. This also applies to the outcomes. The more users there are that believe that the outcomes are due to faulty software, the greater the risk perception.

Figure : Technology Threat Avoidance Model
Source: Adapted from (Liang/Xue 2009, 9)

The other process is the *Coping Appraisal*. The Perceived Avoidability is affected by three components: Perceived effectiveness, Perceived costs and self efficacy. "[P]erceived effectiveness refers to an individual's subjective assessment that the safeguarding measure can effectively avoid the threat of malicious IT. Based on this assessment, users can appraise whether the threat is avoidable" (Liang/Xue 2009, 11). The Costs like money or time are also an important point for the user decision. Self efficacy described the own motivation in heavy situation.

It is only after a threat, as a result of the threat appraisal and coping appraisal process, has been perceived, that the user develops a sense of urgency that motivates themselves to search for information in order to address the threat. This process is called *Coping*. With the TTAT model, he/she follows the process of the IT threat appraisal. There are two ways of coping with threats that can be distinguished: problem-focused coping and emotion-focused coping (Lazarus/Folkman 1984, 187-181). Problem-focused coping entails that a user searches for information about specific concerns in order to overcome the objective problem through action or omission. It also entails that the user does this in order to adapt to the situation. With

26

regard to malware, this can, for example, be the establishment of security measures such as spyware scanners or antivirus scanners, the deactivation of cookies or changing all of the passwords. After taking these measures, the user feels safer. By taking a step to further remove themselves from unwanted threat-based anxiety, the threat itself is in turn reduced.

The second form of coping is emotion-focused coping. It entails dealing with the emotions that are connected to the problem. Emotional stimuli are reduced. An example of this is the reduction of stress or anxiety. Nothing changes with the real problem.

Liang and Xue describe the following procedure in relation to the IT security (Liang/Xue 2009, 1-21). As IT users prefer a rational approach, they will initially go through the problem-oriented coping process. In doing so, they look for various safety measures and choose the option that most greatly reduces the threat. This means that IT security measures present a sub-objective in order to avoid the main objective. The main objective remains preventing IT attacks.

If the user doesn't find a rational protective mechanism or if the selected protection fails, they use emotion-focused coping. Failure is a regular phenomenon with malware because its recognizable features are constantly being changed and concealed. The user therefore tries to subjectively play the risk down.

In summary, it can be said that both emotion-focused coping and problem-oriented coping reduce IT risks to a certain extent.

Liang and Xue (Liang/Xue 2009, 14f) look at two factors that influence the TTAT: risk tolerance and social influence. They define risk tolerance as "the minimum discrepancy between the undesired end state (attacked by malicious IT) and the current state that users are able to tolerate" (Liang/Xue 2009, 14). Thus, a risk-tolerant user accepts more threats than a user who is less tolerant. They sees a lower risk potential in the same threat. Risk tolerance therefore has a negative impact on the IT risk perception.

The second influence on the TTAT is the social environment. The individual user is always surrounded by a group, institution, organization or society. This environment influences them significantly. Liang and Xue distinguish two social influences in this regard (Liang/Xue 2009, 14ff). The first one is informational influence. The IT user's environment presents information that is supposed to help them deal with threats and safety measures. This is particularly important if the user lacks required IT security knowledge. The second social influence is the normative influence. The normative influence is divided into three processes: compliance, internalization, and identification. Compliance is based on the concept of consent, acceptance and remuneration as well as a fear of punishment. Internalization is the consultation process between the values and goals of the individual and the group. Identification describes self-definition in relation to the group. The result of this three-part process is that the individual displays a behavior that is socially required or desired. An example of this is a company employee. They themselves don't recognize the threats of viruses, spyware and so on. However, they will follow the company's IT security policy.

3.2.5 Risk Perception Amongst Managers

Straub (Straub 1990, 1-23) examined the perception of computer abuse in management. Computer abuse by administrators and IT security managers is a two part process (Straub/Nance 1990, 1-17). First, the abuse must be detected. Once an abnormality has been discovered in the system, the offenders have to be identified. Despite the immense consequences and damages caused by computer abuse, IT security is a low priority in the management sector. Straub's empirical study suggests three reasons for this. First, managers consciously choose to invest very little in IT security because they think that the amount of IT abuse that's occurring is low. Second, managers are skeptical about IT security because it is difficult to assess its effectiveness. "Third, managers may lack knowledge about the range of controls available to reduce IS security abuses. To raise management involvement in IS security decisions, it is important to convince managers about the benefits of IS security efforts and let them know what kinds of IS security measures are effective under what organizational circumstances" (Kankanhalli et al. 2003, 2).

"Information security continues to be ignored by top managers, middle managers, and employees alike. The result of this neglect is that organizational systems are far less secure than they might otherwise be and that security breaches are far more frequent and damaging than is necessary" (Straub/Welke 1998, 3).

3.2.6 User Participation in IS Security Risk Management

In IT security literature, the user is seen as a weakness (Siponen 2000, 1-13) (Dhillon/Moores 2001, 1-10). Thus, the user could be both the problem and the problem solver. However, this doesn't always have to be the case. Including the user in the IT security process can also exert a positive influence.

Spears and Barki (Spears/Barki 2010, 1-26) examined the impact of user involvement in the IT Security Risk Management (=SRM) process. 228 people from the information technology governance, auditing and security sectors were interviewed. The investigation is related to the American "Sarbanes Oxley Act". The Sarbanes Oxley Act is a federal U.S. law which was introduced in response to accounting scandals in the U.S. Its objective is to improve the reliability of corporate reporting for the public capital markets. For this purpose, internal controls have to be introduced in the organizations. These controls are to effectively safeguard financial information systems from computer crime, employee errors and other attacks on the financial system. With their implementation in the companies, both IT security and business processes must be adjusted accordingly.

In order to evaluate user participation, a theoretical model of information systems development was used. In information system development, user participation is defined as "the extent to which users or their representatives carry out assignments and perform various activities and behaviors during ISD and conceptualized it along four dimensions: users' hands-on performance of activities, responsibility, relations with IS, and communication with

IS staff and senior management" (Spears/Barki 2010, 2). Markus and Mao (Markus/Mao 2004, 3-9) have proposed three theoretical models that explain how user involvement influences the system's success. They are: buy-in, system quality, and emergent interactions.

The buy-in theory states that participating in and influencing the development of a system has an influence on the experience. The system is viewed as being much more important and personal. Psychological factors change the attitude of the system user.

According to the system quality theory, the quality of a system increases with the inclusion of the user because the developer obtains all of the necessary information about the business requirements. User involvement is especially useful when it comes to dealing with large, complex or conceptually new projects.

The third model, emergent interactions, describes the relationship between developers and users that builds up during the development period. "A "good" relationship is likely to lead to success not only in terms of higher quality systems (because the IS professionals become more likely to consider business needs in their designs), but also in terms of relational and affective outcomes (e.g., higher levels of user and designer satisfaction); in contrast, "bad" relationships that are frequently fraught with conflicts and disputes are likely to lead to less positive outcomes" (Spears/Barki 2010, 3).

The models that are related to the development of information systems can be transferred to security risk management. User involvement not only has a positive influence on the development of information systems, but also on the successful implementation of IT security measures in risk management. "Success" entails minimizing deficits in security risk management while increasing effectiveness.

Spear and Barki illustrate the influence of user involvement with a model The influence of user participation on organizational awareness, business-aligned security risk management and control development was examined (see Figure 5).

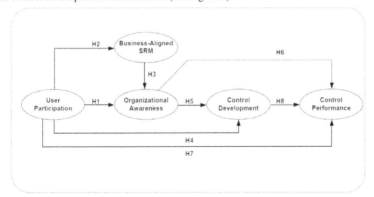

Figure : User Participation in SRM
Source: (Spears/Barki 2010, 12)

User participation is understood as user involvement in general security risk management, control management and accountability. Organizational awareness is structured with an increasing awareness and the improved adoption of IT security policy measures amongst different groups such as end users, IT security specialists or senior management. Business-aligned security Risk Management describes "(1) the extent to which security policies and controls are based on business objectives, value, or needs, and (2) the extent to which business users routinely contribute a business perspective to IT on managing security risk" (Spears/Barki 2010, 13). Control development refers to general security policies such as acceptable and unacceptable behavior, organizational policies and policies such as risk tolerance that are specific to organization.

Figure 5 shows the model with the following hypotheses:

H1: User participation in SRM raises organizational awareness of IS security risks and controls.

H2: User participation contributes to an alignment between SRM and the business context.

H3: Business-aligned SRM contributes to greater organizational awareness of IS security.

H4: User participation contributes to perceive improvements in control development.

H5: Organizational awareness of SRM within a business process contributes to perceived improvements in control development for controls within that business process.

H6: Organizational awareness of SRM within a business process positively influences the perceived performance of security controls.

H7: User participation positively influences the performance of security controls.

H8: Improvements in control development positively influences the performance of security controls.

The following correlations were found. "User participation in SRM was found to raise organizational awareness of security risks and controls within targeted business processes, and facilitated greater alignment of SRM with business objectives, values, and needs" (Spears/Barki 2010, 15). This improves the development and performance of security controls (e.g. access control, segregated duties, security policy).

User participation has the strongest effect on business alignment. In practice, this means that users gain a higher level of security awareness when IT security is something that they can identify with. This occurs when SRM becomes a part of the business process and then actually deals with SRM tasks. Consequently, user participation can be used as a tool to increase the user's risk perception.

In summary, one can say that integrating the user in SRM creates two positive results. On the one hand, it creates an enhanced risk awareness with the user, while on the other hand, security measures can be better adapted to economic objectives. Users therefore bring value to the SRM sector when they are involved in its sub-processes. Security managers can see regulatory provisions such as the Sarbanes Oxley Act as an opportunity. Since the risk awareness of the company and the employees is strengthened and IT security is better able to adapt to the company's goals, IT security measures gain a stronger acceptance.

3.2.7 IT Security From an Entrepreneurial Standpoint

These days, information systems are of the utmost importance when it comes to exploiting strategic advantages and handling managerial tasks. These systems are ever-increasing assets in companies that must therefore be protected accordingly. It is therefore surprising that management pays relatively little attention to IT security in comparison to other sectors (Brancheau/Janz/Wetherbe 1996, 5,16-19).

Dhillon and Backhouse (Dhillon/Backhouse 2000, 1-3) consider the tasks of IT security management to extend much further than mere technical installations. In IT security, we don't need an excessive number of rules that tell us how to behave in a particular situation. What's needed are rules that: a) make constant observation possible; and b) allow us an approach in which no specific requirements exist. According to Dhillon and Blackhouse, IT Security is no longer a technical problem but rather a social, organizational and human problem. Traditional IT policies such as confidentiality, integrity or availability are wonderful as long as they work. Nevertheless, these guidelines are very limited in their application and fields. These three aspects of IT data security can come into conflict with business-related goals. Next, we will consider the issue of confidentiality, integrity and availability more closely.

The data security goal of confidentiality is strongly linked with data access control. However, this comes into conflict with the organizational view that data should be accessible to as many sectors in the company as possible.

"Integrity refers to maintaining the values of the data stored and manipulated, such as maintaining the correct signs and symbols. But what about how these figures are interpreted for use. Businesses need employees who can interpret the symbols processed and stored. We refer not only to the numerical and language skills, but also to the ability to use the data in a way that accords with the prevailing norms of the organization" (Dhillon/Backhouse 2000, 3). For example, the review may help creditworthiness. In this respect, we need correct applicant data and a corresponding interpretation in accordance with business guidelines and legal guidelines. As such, the data and especially its interpretations must be protected.

"Availability" describes the condition that data should always be available when needed. Unlike confidentiality and integrity, availability presents smaller problems for organizations. Dhillon and Backhouse suggest the RITE principles for traditional data security goals. They consist of *r*esponsibility, *i*ntegrity, *t*rust and *e*thicality.

These days, most organizations are spread across the entire globe. The assignment of responsibilities plays an important role with geographically dispersed organizations. In IT security, however, *responsibility* entails much more than just bearing the consequences of a failed project. "So being responsible means not just carrying the can for when something has gone wrong in the past (accountability—for attributing blame) but refers also to handling the development of events in the future in a particular sphere" (Dhillon/Backhouse 2000, 3). If a new situation arises, someone must take on the responsibility without being asked.

The second RITE principle is *integrity*. Data, information and knowledge are the most important resources of a company. Most violations of the IT system come from structures that are found within the system. The loyalty of the employees therefore plays a significant role. The third principle is trust. In today's organizations, self control and responsibility are considered to be more important than trust. Careful trust is less viable in a globalized world.

Trust must therefore be the binding element between the organizations. *Ethicality* is the last RITE principle. This refers to rules or practices that distinguish right from wrong and it doesn't apply to business rules. Business rules are only intended for foreseeable circumstances and therefore don't apply to dynamic situations that are prevalent today. Oftentimes, rules for a particular circumstance don't even exist.

3.2.8 Differences in Computer Ethics

International studies show that people with different backgrounds have different views towards computer ethics. Whitman et al. (Whitman/Townsend/Hendrickson 1999, 1-15 ; Whitman et al. 1998, 1-7) investigated computer ethics in relation to viruses, software license violation (Moores 2003, 1ff ; Gopal/Sanders 2000 1ff; Husted 20001ff) and the abuse of company computer resources. This study was done in nine countries (Singapore, Hong Kong, the United States, Great Britain, Australia, Sweden, Wales and the Netherlands). All countries consider viruses or hacking to be unacceptable behavior. The study showed that there is a difference in tolerance. Singapore and Hong Kong are more tolerant than English-speaking countries (U.S.A., Wales, Great Britain, and Australia). Sweden and the Netherlands are significantly more tolerant than Wales and Australia, but they are also significantly more intolerant than Singapore and Hong Kong. In contrast, Singapore and Hong Kong see the use of a company's computer resources for private purposes as being highly unethical. All other countries see it as legitimate if it has not been expressly prohibited by the company.

"As ethics are a result of one's environmental upbringing, it is important to stress to organizations conducting business internationally, to use caution in placing expectations on the ethical performance of expatriates and foreign nationals without first trying to understand their perspectives, and educating them as to the organization's perspectives. Similarly, organizations operating outside the boundaries of the US and its territories must use caution in dealing with local customs and codes of ethics" (Whitman 2004, 2).

4 Comparison of Risk understanding in Information Systems and Sociology

In comparing the understanding of risk in sociology and information systems, you initially notice the objective notion of risk in information systems. In the field of IT security and project management, security is seen as being ratable and negotiable. "However it is deeply socially constructed and its management goes to the heart of professional identity. In some sectors, the adoption of a new risk management method has segued with an existing risk culture and been reinforced by a sympathetic institutional logic. However, in others the introduction of new categories of risk represents a major transformation in organizational priorities and management practices" (Scott/Perry 2009, 2).

The risk in information systems can be seen as a specific domain. This means that in both the fields of IT security and project management, a specific idea of what constitutes a threat or a risk is conceived. In contrast, the approaches of Beck, Luhmann, Douglas and Foucault follow a more general path. They do not differ according to specific dangers such as budgets or timing in project management. They define general categories such as danger and safety as well as risk and threat. In these general categories, one can classify specific cases such as natural disasters, nuclear accidents and so on.

It is obvious that the understanding of risk in sociology is the surrounding construct of the understanding of risk in information systems. In sociology, the framework of our notion of risk is set. The consequences and their assessments are also based on social elements of human coexistence. Our actions towards certain threats are fundamentally shaped by the social trade. From a sociological point of view, "trade" signifies an active reference to the environment (Meulemann 2006, 29-32). Social trade signifies an action, toleration or omission that the actor links with purposefulness and which has an impact on his/her environment.

In comparison table 1 different views of risk sociology are compared with views from the areas of IT security and project management. Here, we initially have a comparison of the different risk characteristics. Then we look to the culture theory from Douglas. we will convey Douglas' views regarding information systems. In doing so, the grid-group model plays an important role. Next, we will consider Luhmann's systems theory approach. Beck's understanding of the second reflexive modernity carefully describes the development of information systems. Finally, we will discuss the insurance-based approach of Foucault.

	Sociology	Software project	IT Security
Analyze Categories			
Risk characteristics	Not-local, unpredictable, not compensable (Beck 2009, 3f)	Many different risks. Difficult to predict. (Keil, et al. 2000, 1-10; Wallace/Keil 2004, 1-6 ; Schmidt et al. 2001, 1-33)	From inside and outside (Loch/Carr/Warkentin 1992, 4). Difficult to predict (Loch/Carr/Warkentin 1992, 1-15 ; Straub 1990, 1-23)
Culture aspect	Different culture forms with different risk perceptions (Douglas/Wildavsky 1982 ; Dake 1991, 1-20 ; Dake 1992, 1-14)	Different ranking in USA, Finland and Hong Kong (Schmidt/Lyyinen/Keil/Cule 2001, 1-33)	People from different backgrounds with diverse views in relation to risk (Whitman/Townsend/Hendrickson 1999, 1-15)
Risk perception and environment	People create their own risk environment and new technology brings new risks (Beck 2006, 4 ; Beck 2009, 5ff ; Beck 2007)	Risk checklist, analyse frame work, process model and risk response strategies create their own risk environment. We only see risk we define.	With any new IT technology, our scope of action expands while further dangers arise (Dlaminia/Eloffa/Eloffb 2009, 6-9)

Table : Comparison Sociology with Software project and IT Security Risk
Source: Own presentation

4.1   Comparison of Risk Characteristics

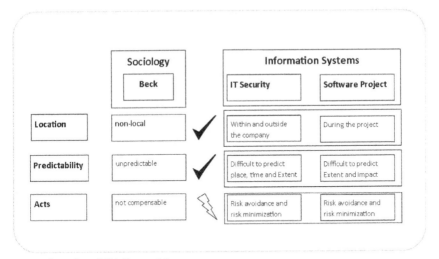

Figure : Comparison of Risk Characteristics
Source: Own presentation

Beck classifies the characteristics of risks as non-local, unpredictable and not compensable (see Figure 6). In IT Security, we have recognized that there is a constant threat that prevails both within and outside of the company. It is very difficult if not impossible for us to determine the timing, location and extent of the danger. Beck's first two classification characteristics – non-local and unpredictable – were recognized in the IT security field. However, the non-compensable characteristic isn't. In the survey of IT managers, a large portion of them felt secure and well prepared for potential attacks. In project management, one also feels secure with the prevailing models and methods for software development. One internally contemplates how to control the risks, which is a sociological mistake.

4.2   The Culture Theory in Information Systems

Douglas describes risk from a fundamentally cultural viewpoint. Cultural aspects such as rules and the environment influence the individual risk perception. Risk perception is formed as a collective construct of society. The interpretation is influenced by social norms. Trade is also socially conditioned.

In the field of IT security research, Liang and Xue (Liang/Xue 2009, 14) found that our perceptions of dangers are guided by social influences. There is a distinction between the informal and normative influence. Liang and Xue (Liang/Xue 2009, 14) also found that an individual always belongs to a group, organization or society. It's precisely with the normative influence that the culture theory comes into play. The normative influence describes the process of compliance, internalization, and identification from the perspective of information systems.

Compliance is based on acceptance or reward. Internalization is the coordination between personal goals and group goals. Identification is the feeling of belonging to a group.

What Liang and Xue (Liang/Xue 2009, 15) understand as "identification", Douglas terms as a "group". Both should clarify the extent to which a person feels like they belong to and identify with a particular group. According to Douglas, the corresponding dimension for a "group" is the grid dimension. The grid indicates the degree to which someone accepts the formal hierarchy and control system of a group. Liang and Xue describe this as "compliance and internalization" (Liang/Xue 2009, 14). Both should clarify the relationship between the individual and the group. One can therefore consider the group and identification pairing as well as the grid and compliance/internalization pairing as being equivalent.

In sociology, the grid group model is used to analyze risk perception and describe the social desirability of the risk. In the grid-group model's original form, Douglas (Douglas/Wildavsky 1982) distinguishes four different social groups:

Entrepreneurs, bureaucrats, atomized individuals and egalitarians.

In building on Douglas' grid-group model, Dake (Dake 1991, 1-20) (Dake 1992, 1-14) developed a model of idealized cultural forms that is derived from the social groups.

They include: individualism, hierarchy, fatalism and egalitarianism.

Individualism corresponds to the entrepreneurs, hierarchy to the bureaucrats, fatalism to the atomized individuals and egalitarianism the egalitarians. In follow we use the declaration individualism, hierarchy, fatalism and egalitarianism. Figure 7 shows examples of different culture forms in the field of IT Security und software project development.

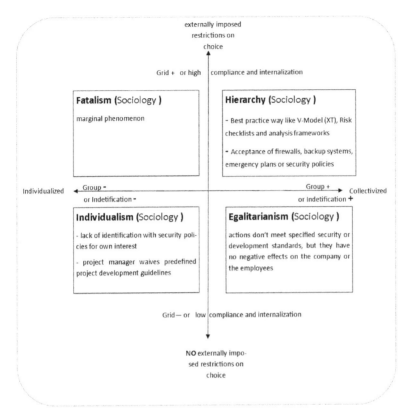

externally imposed
restrictions on
choice

Grid + or high | compliance and internalization

Fatalism (Sociology)

marginal phenomenon

Hierarchy (Sociology)

- Best practice way like V-Model (XT), Risk
checklists and analysis frameworks

- Acceptance of firewalls, backup systems,
emergency plans or security policies

Individualized ← Group -
or Indetification -

Group +
or Indetification +
→ Collectivized

Individualism (Sociology)

- lack of identification with security policies for own interest

- project manager waives predefined
project development guidelines

Egalitarianism (Sociology)

actions don't meet specified security or
development standards, but they have
no negative effects on the company or
the employees

Grid— or low compliance and internalization

NO externally impo-
sed restrictions on
choice

Figure : Culture forms in Information Systems
Source: Own presentation

Individuals groups perceive risk as a chance to become successful in the competitive market
and pursue personal goals. Their group membership (group) is low, while their acceptance of
a hierarchy and rules is also low. "[Risks are necessary costs for the further development and
improvement of one's quality of life]" (Renn 1991).

The question that arises is whether such a group of people can be found in the area of IT
security. As a simple example, you can look at an end user in a company that should change
their password every four weeks for security reasons. This password change can be given as a
security policy from the company. For the sake of convenience or due to forgetfulness, the
employee doesn't accept this password change. This convenience indicates a high interest in
their personal goals. In this case, the feeling of group membership in the company or its
security policy is low. Generally, one can say that the entrepreneurial group represents those
individuals who have set a low sense of identification with the company or the safety
guidelines. The lack of identification with security policies may be attributed to an ignorance

37

of their meaning and relevance. However, it can also be related to a lack of knowledge about proper usage. Spear and Barki show that the inclusion of end users in the risk management process indicates the users' risk awareness. The acceptance of the policies is thereby increased. This leads to a higher grid. In addition, by integrating the user, the community spirit can be increased for security measure necessities. Thus, the group dimension is increased.

In the area of project management, one could imagine the following scenario: In order to successfully complete a project, the project manager waives predefined project development guidelines. In order to remain within the plan's timeline, for example, the required engineering phase is shortened. The project manager therefore takes the risk of developing a product that doesn't satisfy the requirements of the customer. In the crop group of entrepreneurs, risk is perceived as an opportunity.

The second group is the *hierarchy*. They are characterized by a high degree of group affiliation and a high acceptance of the formal hierarchy and control system. This control system has mainly been created by experts. In a group, risks are perceived as being harmless or natural when dangers can in fact be blocked by the existing system. This is especially predominant in project management. The software development process is strictly set through development proposals, development models such as a spiral model, V-models or V-models XT. Risk checklists and analysis frameworks are supposed to uncover potential risks on time. Risk strategy, risk identification, risk analysis, risk responses and risk control form the hierarchy and control system. These control systems attempt to control possible risks and determine reactions to certain risks. As such, the hierarchy group - and in this case, the software developers – feels safe enough to place a great deal of confidence in the given expert system.

A similar situation prevails in the field of IT security. Through introduced security measures such as firewalls, backup systems, emergency plans or security policies, a control system is designed to be largely accepted by the employees. There is confidence in this.

Fatalistic cultural manifestations occur through a high level of external control with existing group exclusion. They only believe in the existing hierarchy system. Like egalitarians, fatalists are a marginal phenomenon that in reality is very rare. It's difficult to imagine a comparative cultural situation in a company. The specified control system would have to be so distinct that the individual would have no means to reach a decision on their own. Furthermore, there is no connection and integration with the group, which in our case is the company. The risk is considered to be inevitable and can only be avoided with luck (Renn 1991).

The *Egalitarianism* group describes the way of life of one of the partners in the cooperation as being more important than individual goals at a low level of hierarchy acceptance. Solidarity, group membership and the equality of group members are especially important to the individual. Risks are perceived as an external threat. Due to the lack of a control system and expert knowledge, socially acceptable solutions are sought after. In literature, this crop group is often also referred to as a sect. When transferred to the field of information systems, these actions don't meet specified security or development standards, but they have no negative effects on the company or the employees. When confronted with risks, reliable measures for the community are favored over a personal or corporate gain.

In summary, the sociological cultural forms can be found in the company again. A company therefore forms its own risk culture that the employees act upon. Both the group bond (group) and hierarchy or control system (grid) dimensions play a crucial role in this case. One can assume that most members strongly identify with their duties and their companies. The value of the group dimension is so high. In project management, each employee develops their own identity with the project. This identification with the project and the common goal of successfully completing a project leads to a high group formation. In the area of project management, however, one speaks less of groups and more of teams, working groups or project groups. With a highly trained community spirit, there are two possible characteristics of cultural form: Hierarchy and Egalitarianism . The egalitarians are a fringe group in both the social world and in business. In project management, the primary goal is to hold the quality of the product and the process at a high standard. This objective is more important to the employee than subordinated personal or group-based goals. Consequently, it is rather rare to find the cultural form of egalitarians in project management. The crop group that project management generally finds itself in is that of the Hierarchie. Identifying with one's teammates, good cooperation and concerted action are the cornerstones of project development. From a sociological point of view, a high degree of group affiliation is present. The development of software projects is surrounded by a system of rules. Scientific studies and industry experience have led to various best practice models of software development, which are accepted and applied. There is a similar situation that prevails in the area of IT security. Security systems and policies form the rule system that is recommended by experts and scientists. The cultural form of bureaucrats therefore prevails to the greatest extent possible in software project management and IT security. "[Within this group, risks are then classified as acceptable if there are sufficient, institutionally solidified routines to determine and control these risks]" (Renn 1991, 200).

However, it should be noted that a general classification of project management and IT security that's based on cultural form is difficult. This is because the personal views of employees and the company's understanding and approach to risk are too different.

Schmidt et al. (Schmidt et al. 2001, 1-33) found that the view and ranking of project risks differs between the USA, Finland and Hong Kong. Whiteman (Whitman/Townsend/Hendrickson 1999, 1-15) et al. reached a similar conclusion regarding IT security. These are people from different backgrounds with diverse views in relation to viruses, software licenses and the misuse of company computer resources. This illustrates that although the risks are identical throughout the world, a different perception prevails. This can be explained through the cultural differences. Douglas believes that culture has a greater influence on risk perception than one's personal attitude toward risk.

Social risks are formed through ethical and moral constructs. Since ethics and morals are different from country to country, there are different conceptions of risk.

The employees are influenced by ethical and moral constructs. There are also business objectives on top of that. As a result, the company faces different risks. These identified risks are combated with the help of risk management. The process of risk management consists of identifying, analyzing and handling the risk. During both the identification of and analysis of risks, these ethical and moral constructs influence the employees. Consequently, the conclusion is that the danger level of the same risks in software project management and IT security are perceived differently in different countries. This connection is shown once again in Figure 8.

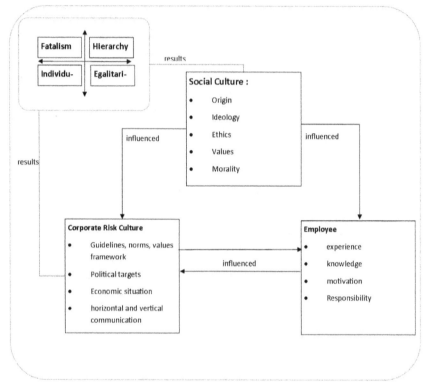

Figure : Influence of Social and Corporate Risk Culture on the Employee
Source: Own presentation

At the top level, we have the *Social culture* in which the individual and the company reside. Every culture has its own ideology, ethics and values. At this cultural level, established habits, customs and practices influence people greatly without their even knowing it. This level of culture can be analyzed with Douglas' grid-group model and an appropriate cultural form can then be found.

The second level is *corporate risk culture* (Schlienger/Teufel 2003) (Ngo/Zhou/Warren 2005, 1-4). Risk culture is understood to be a common standard and value-based structure of the management and members of a company. All employees must develop an awareness of risks. Through this awareness, a targeted and controlled perception of risk comes into being. "[Information security should become a part of our daily lives; it should be as natural as security for transport or buildings]" (Schlienger/Teufel 2007, 4). "In a well-controlled organization with an institutionalized risk management culture, however, employees will do the right thing even in the face of unclear policies. Organizations that establish a strong risk management culture will foster risk-informed decision making that ensures its long-term viability" (Cooper 2010, 1) . With reference to Figure 8 and in the context of corporate risk culture, guidelines, norms and values that are created in relation to company-based risk are initially summarized. These can be influenced by political objectives or the economic situation. Even the horizontal and vertical communication about risks in the company is part of the established risk culture. As with the outer level, the cultural risk level can be similarly analyzed with the help of the grid group dimensions. This results in a so-called entrepreneurial culture form.

The third level is the *employee* himself. He is influenced by the social cultural level as well as the corporate risk culture level. The employee acts in accordance with the ethical and moral values of the social cultural level, but is influenced by the specified rules of the company. In addition, there are psychological factors such as experience, knowledge and motivation involved. Concern, competence and responsibility play an important role with the employee. All of these described factors create the perceived risk. Since culture and risk culture differ from country to country and from company to company, there are different perceptions of risk. For example, this can lead to differences when using foreign computer resources or assessing project risks. These differing risk perceptions are the basis for why a company's policies, standards and value structure – i.e. risk culture – are adapted to the perceived risk.

Renn (Renn 1991, 9).argues that a communication between the four - and in his opinion, five - different culture forms (individualism, hierarchy, fatalism, egalitarianism) is rarely achieved, "[because the respective groups' patterns of perception and images of reality are not compatible]" (Renn 1991, 9). Consequently, the corporate risk culture must adapt to the surrounding outer culture. If they do not conform to one another, "[they will permanently talk at cross-purposes]" (Renn 1991, 9).

4.3   Risk Perception, Risk Environment and Risk Transformation

Luhmann argues that risk perception and its acceptance are dependent on the assessment of the individual. The individual perceives an incident as a risk or a danger. In addition, the assessment of the incident is influenced by whether the individual is the decision maker or the affected person. March and Shapira (March/Shapira 1987, 1-15), Schmidt et al. (Schmidt et al. 2001, 1-33), Straub Straub (Straub 1990, 1-23) found that the classification of potential dangers with IT security risks is low all the way from different levels of management through to the workers. The assessment of IT security risks depends on whether I am the decision maker or the affected person. As long as I only have to decide on protective measures, I tend to have a lower risk rating. Once the danger arrives, I sway into the role of the affected person and rank the level of risk as being much greater. A similar situation can be found in software project management. The classification of the risks is significantly influenced by the degree of control. The less control a project manager has over a risk, the more they will classify it as being risky. As long as the project manager has sufficient control over the course of the project, they will find themselves in the role of the decision maker. They are in a position to be significantly influenced during the course of the project. Luhmann describes this situation as being a security illusion. This is understood as rational thinking building a sense of security, which in reality doesn't exist. IT security floats in this illusion of security as well. Through the use of security systems and measures, the person believes that they are protected. They rely on these measures and are therefore in a situation of being the decision maker; they aren't in the dramatic situation that the affected person perceives.

Another viewpoint that Luhmann introduces is the difference between risk and safety as well as risk and danger. In most scientific works in the area of IT security and software project risks, the main topics are risk and safety. Especially in the IT security field, the concept of security is of the utmost importance. All activities are designed to make the existing system more secure. Luhmann calls this the illusion of safety. Through facts and their interpretation, a self-designed security environment is formed which aims to maximize the given security. According to Luhmann, there is no such thing as absolute security because decisions are linked to the impact of an uncertain future. This in turn means that we can develop and use as many checklists, analysis models, process models and best practice plans as we want, but we will never reach a level of complete security. Each of these measures is only increases the illusion of safety.

Instead of talking about risk and safety, Luhmann proposes making a distinction between risk and danger. Risk should be seen as the attribution to a form of damage that is caused by one's personal decision or omission. Danger is the attribution of the damage to the external environment.

Making this classification in Whitman's IT (Whitman 2004, 7) security ranking, results in the following classifications.

Risks are therefore deliberate software attacks, act of human error or failure, deliberate acts of theft, compromises to intellectual property, quality of service deviations from service providers, technological obsolescence and deliberate acts of information extortion. Dangers are technical software failures or errors, deliberate acts of espionage or trespass, deliberate acts of sabotage or vandalism, technical hardware failures or errors and forces of nature.

Risk transformation is a process in which a danger is converted into a risk. For example, technically related software errors or hardware failures can be converted into a risk by using monitoring tools. Based on the allocation of the damage to the external environment, the former risk is transformed to an individual decision. In the field of IT security and project management, one feels safer if risks are controllable. We will therefore constantly attempt to convert dangers into manageable risks. The table 2 shows different IT Security Risk from Whiteman (Whitman 2004, 7). In the first column we saw the Risk. The second column shows if a Risk transformation is possible.

IT Security Risk Ranking from Whiteman	Risk transformation from Danger to Risk possible?
Deliberate software attacks	Yes
Technical software failures or errors	Partially
Act of human error or failure	Partially
Deliberate acts of espionage or trespass	No
Deliberate acts of sabotage or vandalism	No
Technical hardware failures or errors	No
Deliberate acts of theft	Partially
Forces of nature	No
Compromises to intellectual property	No
Quality of service deviations from service providers	Yes
Technological obsolescence	Yes
Deliberate acts of information extortion	No

Table : IT Security Risk Transformation
Source: Own presentation

In doing so, however, we lose sight of the fact that nothing has changed with the original risk. The probability of risk remains the same, but our idea of the risk has changed.

In order to carry out the process of transforming dangers to risks, preventative measures are used as according to Luhmann. We want to guard against preventative hardware failures with the monitoring tool. In project management, the project leader constantly tries to collect information on progress in order to keep the project under control. Luhmann describes this behavior as a risk diversification strategy. At the beginning of the project, the project leader reached a decision that he wasn't sure of. In order to confirm this decision, he takes the preventative measures of project monitoring. In doing so, however, he ignores the fact that monitoring only serves to confirm his first decision. As such, a pseudo-controllability is created. The first decision and thereby risk is distributed across various measures with the aim of getting a confirmation of the initial decision.

Looking at the surroundings in which we encounter risks, we come to the approach of Beck which is retrievable in information systems. Beck's basic assumption is that the individual creates their own risk environment and must therefore deal with it. In the historical reflection of IT security, you realize just that. With any new technology, our scope of action expands while further dangers arise. In the early days of computers, only one physical backup was needed. The system had to be protected against foreign users and theft. With the introduction of the remote backup, the risk environment eventually changed once again. The pure physical backup is no longer adequate. The remote data must be protected. This was done by means of authentication and identification methods. The creation of new technologies results in new ways to for them to be attacked. As such, the struggle in defending against these new threats is the fundamental problem in the field of IT security.

Even the risk environment is self-created with regard to project management. The manner in which the project should be carried out is already determined during the requirements review. By collecting data from different requirement factors, a common understanding is presented on the one hand, while on the other hand; clear limits are set with regard to failure. If the specified requirements are either not met or met in a manner that's different than planned, there is a risk that we are the cause of it. Beck's opinion that we only recognize risks that we've previously identified is a good reflection of this. The environment in which we find ourselves and our systems is subject to constant change. The risks grow. Beck's term of reflexive modernity therefore also applies to information systems because we create our own risks and then try to deal with them.

Finally, we consider the views of Foucault. For him and his scientific staff, risk is predictable. In this connection, Foucault goes one step further than Beck and Luhmann. Risks are not only the nature of technology or society, but also a specific type of social thinking about events. Upon closer examination of his views, one notices that the signs are quite plausible and true to reality, but they don't present any actual additional value for the information systems. Only the idea of risk is to be regarded as an opportunity and the key message is that technologies of power should be used instead of the power of technology. The key message implies that we should have less to do with technology itself and more to do with the possibilities of regulation and control – i.e. the handling – in order to create a more interesting approach. However, Foucault doesn't get into exactly how this should be executed.

5   Discussion and Outlook

In closing, one can say that the sociology of risk sets the framework in which IT security and project management act. The understanding of what IT and project risks are and how we perceive them is set in the social structures. In this connection, Douglas' culture theory plays a crucial role. The culture and therefore the origin, ethics, values and beliefs of every individual significantly influences what we consider to be a risk and how strongly the threat affects our society. However, we don't consciously perceive this influence.

A company can be seen as a small, individual culture. This culture can be described as an entrepreneurial risk culture. Even in this risk culture, there are guidelines under which we act. What is seen as a risk for the company has implications and consequences for ourselves. The risk culture presents rules on a small scale that nevertheless defines the culture at large. Further studies must test just how closely risk culture and culture are linked. The dependencies and influences need to be looked into. One needs to ask how the risk culture should be designed in a company so that it doesn't come into conflict with the sociological culture. In the sociological culture, the majority of a group's members experience the same incidents as threats or risks. This awareness is missing with regard to IT security. Often, only the IT security department is aware of the real dangers. This awareness is missing at both the management and employee levels. By creating a common awareness, the entrepreneurial risk culture can have a shared vision and awareness with regard to risks. The sociological concept of safety culture may be helpful in achieving this.

Furthermore, the sociological view of the safety illusion and risk diversification strategy generally isn't found in information systems. The actual knowledge that IT security risks and project risks can be managed so that they don't arise is an illusion. Though information systems know that complete security doesn't exist, one nevertheless feels safe enough with the existing provisions. There is also a view that models, risk checklists and so on only distribute the risk. The question is how both of these ideas can be implemented in the risk management process and what benefits they actually bring.

List of Cited Literature

Asselt, MBAV; Vos, E (2008): Wrestling with uncertain risks: EU regulation of GMOs and the uncertainty paradox. In: Journal of Risk Research, Vol. 11 Nr. 1-2, S. 281–300.

Bagchi, K.; Udo, G. (2003): An Analysis of the growth of computer and internet security breaches. In: Communications of the Association for Information Systems, Vol. 12 , 684-700.

Bannerman, P.L. (2008): Risk and risk management in software projects: A reassessment. In: The Journal of Systems and Software , Vol. 81 , S. 2118–2133.

Baraki, H.; Rivard, S.; Talbot, J. (2001): An Integrative Contingency Model of Software Project Risk Management. In: Journal of Management Information Systems, Vol. 17 Nr. 4, 37-69.

Beck, U. (1986): Risikogesellschaft. Auf dem Weg in eine andere Moderne. Stuhrkamp Verlag, Frankfurt am Main 1986.

Beck, U. (1999): World risk society. Wiley-Blackwell, Malden 1999.

Beck, U. (2006): Living in the world risk. In: Economy and Society , Vol. 35 Nr. 3, 329-345.

Beck, U. (2007): 'Weltrisikogesellschaft und neuer Kosmopolitismus: die alte Frage', München.

Beck, U. (2009): Risk Society's 'Cosmopolitan Moment'. In: New Geographies 1: After Zero, Vol. 1 , 24-35.

Bergmans, A. (2008): Meaningful communication among experts and affected citizens on risk:challenge or impossibility? In: Journal of Risk Research, Vol. 11 Nr. 1-2, S. 175–193.

Boehm, B. W. (1989): Software Risk Management. In: Lecture Notes in Computer Science, Vol. 387 , 1-19.

Boehm, B. W. (1991): Software risk management: principles and practices. In: IEEE Software, Vol. 8 Nr. 1, 32-41.

Boehm, B. W.; Ross, R. (1989): Theory-W software project management principles and examples. In: IEEE Transactions on Software Engineering, Vol. 15 Nr. 7, 902-916.

Brancheau, J.C. ; Janz, B. D. ; Wetherbe, J. C. (1996): Key Issues in Information Systems Management: 1994-95 SIM Delphi Results. In: MIS Quaneriy, Vol. 20 Nr. 2, 225-242.

Brockhaus, R. H. (1980): Risk, taking propensity of entrepreneurs. In: The Academy of Management Journa, Vol. 23 Nr. 3, 509-520.

Burchell, G.; Gordon, C.; Miller, P. (1991): Governmentality : The Foucault Effect: Studies in Governmentality. University of Chicago Press , London 1991.

Cabano, S. L. (2004): Do We Truly Understand Project Risk? In: AACE International Transactions , 1-6.

Carver, C. S. ; White, T. L. (1994): Behavioral Inhibition, Behavioral Activation, and Affective Responses to Impending Reward and Punishment: The BIS/BAS Scales. In: Journal of Personality and Social Psychology, Vol. 67 Nr. 2, 319-333.

Caulkins, D. D. (1999): Is Mary Douglas's Grid/Group Analysis Useful for Cross-Cultural Research? In: Cross-Cultural Research, Vol. 33 , 108 - 128.

Charette, R. N. (2005): Why software fails? In: IEEE Spectrum, Vol. 42 Nr. 9, S. 42–49.

Cooper, T. (2010): Risk Culture's Driven by IT. In: Bank Technology New, Vol. 23 Nr. 7, 30-30.

Dake, K. (1991): Orienting Dispositions in the Perception of Risk - An Analysis of Contemporary Worldviews and Cultural Biases. In: Journal of Cross-Cultural Psychology, Vol. 22 Nr. 1, 61-82.

Dake, K. (1992): Myths of Nature: Culture and the Social Construction of Risk. In: Issue, Vol. 48 Nr. 4, S. 21–37.

Dean, M. (1998): Mitchell Dean. In: Risk, Calculable and Incalculable, Vol. 49 Nr. 1, 25-42.

Dean, M. (1999): Governmentality: power and rule in modern society. Sage , London 1999.

Dhillon, G.; Backhouse, J. (2000): Information System Security Management in the New Millennium. In: Communication of the ACM, Vol. 43 Nr. 7, 125-128.

Dhillon, G.; Moores, S. (2001): Computer crimes: theorizing about the Enemy Within,". In: Computers & Security, Vol. 20 Nr. 8, 715-723.

Dlaminia, M.T. ; Eloffa, J.H.P. ; Eloffb, M.M. (2009): Information security: The moving target. In: computers & security, Vol. 28 , S. 189– 198.

Douglas, M. (1966): Purity and Danger. An Analysis of Concepts of Pollution and Taboo. Routledge, New York 1966.

Douglas, M. (1978): Cultural Bias. Royal Anthropological Institute, London 1987.

Douglas, M. (2002): Natural Symbols: Explorations in Cosmology. Routledge, London 1996.

Douglas, M.; Wildavsky, A. B. (1982): Risk and culture: An essay on the selection of technical and environmental dangers. University of california press, London 1983.

Ekberg, M. (2007): The Parameters of the Risk Society: A Review and Exploration. In: Current Sociology, Vol. 55 Nr. 3, S. 343.

Elliot, A. J. (2006): The Hierarchical Model of Approach-Avoidance Motivation. In: Motivation and Emotion, Vol. 30 Nr. 2, 111-116.

Ewald, F. (1993): Der Vorsorgestaat. Stahlkamp, Frankfurt am Main 1993.

Goodhue, D.L. ; Straub, D. W. (1991): Security concerns of system users - A study of perceptions of the adequacy of security. In: Information & Management, Vol. 13 , 13-27.

Gopal, R. D.; Sanders, G. L. (2000): Global software piracy: You can't get blood out of a turnip. In: Communications of the ACM, Vol. 43 Nr. 9, 82 - 89.

Hazel, T. (2006): Critical risks in outsourced IT projects: the intractable and the unforeseen. In: Communication of the ACM, Vol. 49 Nr. 11, 75-79.

Husted, B. W. (2000): The Impact of National Culture on Software Piracy. In: Journal of Business Ethics, Vol. 26 Nr. 3, S. 197–211.

Hynuk, S.; Benoit, R.; Mario, B.; Robert, P. (2009): Risk management applied to projects, programs, and portfolios. In: International Journal of Managing Projects in Business, Vol. 2 Nr. 1, 14-35.

Iacovou, C.; Nakatsu, R. (2008): A risk profile of offshore-outsourced development projects. In: Communications of the ACM, Vol. 51 Nr. 6, 89-94.

Iversen, J. H. ; Mathiassen, L. ; Nielsen, P. A. (2004): Managing Risk in Software Process Improvement: An Action Research Approach. In: MIS Quarterly, Vol. 28 Nr. 3, 395-433.

Kalle L.; Mathiassen, L. ; Ropponen, J. (1998): Attention Shaping and Software Risk—A Categorical Analysis of Four Classical Risk Management Approaches. In: Information System Research, Vol. 9 Nr. 3, 233-255.

Kankanhalli, A.; Teo, H.; Tan, B. C. Y. ; Wei, K. K. (2003): An integrative study of information systems security effectiveness. In: International Journal of Information Management, Vol. 23 Nr. 2, S. 139–154.

Keil, M; Cule, P. E. ; Lyytinen, K. ; Schmidt, R. C. (1998): A framework for identifying software project risks. In: Communications of the ACM , Vol. 41 Nr. 11, S. 76–83.

Keil, M. ; Wallace, L. ; Turk, D. ; Dixon-Randall, G. ; Nulden, U. (2000): An investigation of risk perception and risk propensity on the decision to continue a software development project. In: The Journal of Systems and Software, Vol. 53 , 145-157.

Köhler, B. (2006): Soziologie des neuen Kosmopolitismus. Springer, Wiesbaden 2006.

Krohn, W. ; Krücken, G. (1993): Riskante Technologien: Reflexion und Regulation - Einführung in dies sozialwissenschaftliche Risikoforschung. Suhrkamp, Frankfurt a.M 1993.

Lazarus, R. S. ; Folkman, S. (1984): Stress, Coping, and Adaptation. Springer, New York 1994.

Lemke, T. (2000): Neoliberalismus, Staat und Selbsttechnologien. Ein kritischer Überblick über die governmentality studies. In: Politische Vierteljahreszeitschrift, Vol. 41 , 31-47.

Lemke, T. (2002): Foucault, Governmentality, and Critique. In: Rethinking Marxism, Vol. 14 Nr. 3, 49-64.

Lemke, T. (2003): Die Regierung genetischer Risiken. In: Gen-Ethischer Informationsdienst Nr. 161, 3-5.

Lemke, T. (2006): Michel Foucault's political theory of governmentalit. In: Proceedings of Georgian Academy of Sciences, Series in Philosophy, Vol. 1 , 122-138.

Lewis, W. ; Watson, R. T. ; Pickren, A. (2003): An Empirical Assessment of IT Disaster Risk. In: Communications of the ACM, Vol. 46 Nr. 9, 201-205.

Liang, H. ; Xue, Y. (2009): Avoideance of information technolgoy threats: A theoretical perspective. In: MIS Quarterly, Vol. 33 Nr. 1, 71-91.

Loch, K. D. ; **Carr, H. H.** ; **Warkentin, M. E.** **(1992):** Threats to Information Systems:Today's Reality, Yesterday's Understanding. In: MIS Ouarterly, Vol. 16 Nr. 2, 173-186.

Luhmann, N. **(1991):** Soziologie des Risikos. Walter de Gruyter, Berlin 1991.

Luhmann, N. **(2003):** Soziologie des Risikos. Walter de Gruyter, Berlin 2003.

Lupton, D. **(1999):** Risk. Routledge, New York 1999.

Lyytinen, K. ; **Mathiassen, L.** ; **Ropponen, J.** **(1996):** Framework For Software Risk Management. In: Scandinavian Journal of Information Systems, Vol. 8 Nr. 1, S. 53–68.

Maccrimmon, K. R. ; **Wehrung, D. A** . **(1985):** A portfolio of risk measures. In: Theory and Decision, Vol. 19 Nr. 1, 1-29.

March, J.G. ; **Shapira, Z** .**(1987):** Managerial perspectives on risk and risk taking. In: Management Science, Vol. 33 Nr. 11, S. 1404–1418.

Markus, M. L. ; **Mao, J. Y.** **(2004):** Participation in Development and Implementation—Updating an Old, Tired Concept for Today's IS Contexts. In: Journal of the Association for Information Systems, Vol. 5 Nr. 11/12, 514-544.

Metzner, A. **(2002):** Die Tücken der Objekte: über die Risiken der Gesellschaft und ihre Wirklichkeit. Campus , Frankfurt am Main 2002.

Meulemann, H. **(2006):** Soziologie von Anfang an: Eine Einführung in Themen, Ergebnisse und Literatur. VS Verlag für Sozialwissenschaften, Wiesbaden 2006.

Moores, T. T. **(2003):** The Effect of National Culture and Economic Wealth on Global Software Piracy Rates. In: Communications of the ACM , Vol. 46 Nr. 9, 207-215.

Münch, R. **(2002):** Die Zweite Moderne: Realität oder Fiktion? In: Kölner Zeitschrift für Soziologie und Sozialpsychologie , Vol. 54 Nr. 3, 418-443.

Ngo, L. ; **Zhou, W.** ; **Warren, M.** **(2005):** Understanding Transition towards Information Security Culture Change.

Nidumolu, S. **(1995):** The Effect of Coordination and Uncertainty on Software Project Performance: Residual Performance Risk as an Intervening Variable. In: Information Systems Research, Vol. 6 Nr. 3, 191-219.

Parsons, T. **(1991):** The Social System. Routledge sociology classics, London 1991.

Pearce, F. ; **Tombs, S.** **(1996): Hegemony, risk and governance . In: Economy and Society, Vol. 25 Nr. 3, 428-454.**

Pellegrinelli, S. **(1997):** Programme management: organising project-based change. In: International Journal of Project Management, Vol. 15 Nr. 3, 141-149.

Plapp, T. **(2004):** Wahrnehmung von Risiken aus Naturkatastrophen: eine empirische Untersuchung in sechs gefährdeten Gebieten Süd- und Westdeutschlands. Verlag Versicherungswirtschaft,.

Renn, O. **(1991):** Risikokommunikation : Bedingungen und Probleme eines rationales Diskurses über die Akzeptabilität von Risiken in Risiko und Sicherheit technischer Systeme. Birkhäuser, Basel 1991.

Renn, O. (**1991**): Risikowahrnehmung und Risikobewertung: Soziale Perzeption und gesellschaftliche Konflikte in ganzeinheitliche Risikobetrachtungen. Technische, ethische und soziale Aspekte. In: TÜV Rheinland.

Schlienger, T. ; Teufel, S. (**2007**): Informationssicherheit braucht eine Kultur Teil 1. In: BSI Forum, Vol. 1 , 65-68.

Schmidt, R. ; Lyyinen, K. ; Keil, M. ; Cule, P. (**2001**): Identifying Software Project Risks: An International Delphi Study. In: Joumat of Management Information Systems, Vol. 17 Nr. 4,. 5-36.

Schwarz, M. ; Thompson, M. (**1990**): Divided We Stand: Redefining Politics, Technology and Social Choice. Library of congress cataloging-in-publication data, Pennsylvania 1990.

Scott, S. ; Perry, N. (**2009**): The enactment of risk categories: The role of information systems in organizing and re-organizing risk management practices in the energy industry. In: Information Systems Frontiers, Vol. 1387-3326 , 1-17.

Siponen, M. T. (**2000**): Critical analysis of different approaches to minimizing user-related faults in information systems security: implications for research and practice. In: Information Management & Computer Security, Vol. 8 Nr. 5, 197-209.

Spears, J. L. ; Barki, H. (**2010**): User Participation in IS Security Risk Management. In: MIS Quarterly, Vol. 34 Nr. 3, 503-522.

Straub, D. W. (**1990**): Effective IS security: An empirical study. In: Information Systems Research, Vol. 1 Nr. 3, S. 55–276.

Straub, D. W.; Nance, W. D. (**1990**): Discovering and Disciplining Computer Abuse in Organizations: A Field Study. In: MIS Quarterly, Vol. 14 Nr. 1, 45-60.

Straub, D. W. ; Welke, R. J. (**1998**): Coping with systems risk: Security planning models for management decision. In: MIS Quarterly, Vol. 22 Nr. 4, S. 441–469.

Tacke, V. (**2000**): Das Risiko der Unsicherheitsabsorption - Ein Vergleich konstruktivistischer Beobachtungsweisen des BSE-Risikos. In: Zeitschrift für Soziologie, Vol. 29 Nr. 2, S. 83–102.

Tsetlin, I. ; Winkler, R. L. (**2005**): Risky Choices and Correlated Background Risk. In: Managment Science, Vol. 51 Nr. 9, S. 1336–1345.

Turnera, J. R.; Müller, R. (**2003**): On the nature of the project as a temporary organization. In: International Journal of Project Management, Vol. 21 Nr. 1, 1-8.

Valverde, M. (**2007**): Genealogies of European states: Foucauldian reflections. In: Economy and Society, Vol. 36 Nr. 1, 159-178.

Vaughan, B. (**2002**): Cultured punishments: The promise of grid-group theory. In: Theoretical Criminolog, Vol. 61 , 411 - 431.

Vleka, C. ; Stalle, P. J. (**1980**): Rational and personal aspects of risk. In: Acta Psychologica, Vol. 45 Nr. 1-3, 273-300.

Wallace, L. ; Keil, M. (**2004**): Software project risks and their effect on outcomes. In: Communications of the ACM , Vol. 47 Nr. 4, 68-73.

Whitman, M. (2004): In defense of the realm: understanding the threats to information security. In: International Journal of Information Management, Vol. 24 Nr. 1, S. 43–57.

Whitman, M. E.; Townsend, A. M. ; Hendrickson, A. R. (1999): Cross-national Differences in Computer-use Ethics: A Nine-country Study. In: Journal of International Business Studies, Vol. 30 Nr. 4, 673-687.

Wiener, N. (1965): Cybernetics or control and communication in the animal and the machine. MIT Press, Cambridge 1965.

Yates, J. (2001): An Interview with Ulrich Beck on Freak and Risk Society. In: The Hedgehog Review, Vol. 4.

Zhang, H. (2007): redefinition of the project risk process: using vulnerability to open up the event-consequence link. In: International Journal of Project, Vol. 25 Nr. 7, S. 694–701.